# BAR WITH A MISSIONARY HEART

## BY

## C. BARTON CARTER

*Barton Carter*

*Luke 1:37*

All Scripture quotations are taken from the King James Version.

**Barefoot Boy With a Missionary Heart**

Copyright @ 2018 by

C. Barton Carter Publisher

9326 E 113th St N

Owasso, Oklahoma 74055

Printed in the United States of America

# TABLE OF CONTENTS

Chapter 1    The Little Barefoot Boy.............................. 1

Chapter 2    The Family ................................................ 10

Chapter 3    Bible College ............................................ 16

Chapter 4    Internship and Deputation ........................ 20

Chapter 5    Philippine Islands ..................................... 26

Chapter 6    First Furlough ........................................... 56

Chapter 7    Philippines Second Term............................ 64

Chapter 8    Second Furlough........................................ 81

Chapter 9    Philippines Third Term............................... 85

Chapter 10   Third Furlough........................................... 93

Chapter 11   The Navajo Reservation ............................ 96

Chapter 12   Second Term on Reservation.................... 113

Chapter 13   After the Mission Field............................. 127

Appendix     Pictures .................................................. 141

# BAREFOOT BOY WITH A MISSIONARY HEART

## Chapter 1 – **The Little Barefoot Boy**

The big, white, fluffy clouds were floating lazily across a deep blue sky. The soft, southerly breeze coming from the Gulf of Mexico was causing the shadows of the clouds to drift across the fields of cotton and grain. The cotton was just beginning to bloom, but the grain was almost ready for the harvest. Lying partially under the shade of a mesquite tree there on a farm in central Texas was a little barefoot boy.

About 10 years old, this little boy was typical of the other farm boys around the countryside. He was wearing striped overalls that had already seen better days. They were faded and had patches sewed on the knees. His face was freckled by many days out in the sun either working or playing. His name was Barton Carter, the son of Clarence and Myrtie Carter. Back at the house, he had a little four-year-old sister, Mary Joyce.

It was a good life on the farm even though the work was hard, and the hours were long. The rewards were abundant. The baby chicks that were bought that spring were now frying size, and Barton had just had a good noon meal of southern fried chicken, hot homemade biscuits, creamed potatoes, and many other fresh vegetables out of the family garden. All of it washed down with several glasses of fresh milk from the five cows Barton helped his Dad milk every morning and every evening.

What do little boys think about when they are lying under a tree watching the clouds float by? Many thoughts were in Barton's head: Wouldn't it be nice to just sit on one of those fluffy clouds and look down at the country side as it floated along? Would sitting on one of those clouds be like sitting on a big pile of cotton that had just been picked? Most people would be surprised at the thoughts that go through little boys' heads. Barton was also thinking: Where did I come from? Why am I here? What is my destiny in life? Little did he realize what God really had in store for him.

You may wonder how I know what was in the mind of that little barefoot boy. You see, I was that little boy.

My dad, Clarence "Bill" Carter had married my mother, Myrtie Fellers on July 5th, 1927. A year and a half later, on January 17, 1929, I was born, a big eleven pound bouncing baby boy. Their only other child, Mary Joyce, was born on December 28th, 1935.

My first grade of school was in a little one-room schoolhouse, where one teacher taught all the grades, way out in the country. I was only 5 years old when I started, I had lots of colds that first year, and I only attended class six months out of that first year. How I passed I will never know. That was the last year for that little one-room school. The next year, the school was consolidated into the Moody School District and everyone was transferred to the school at Moody, Texas. My first few months at the Moody school was a disaster. About all I had learned at the country school was how to write my name. I had never even seen an indoor toilet, much less know how to flush one. It took a while, but a good teacher with a good leather strap caught me up with the rest of my class.

To get to the school in Moody, I had to walk about a mile (most of the time in the mud) and then to stand in the cold and sometimes the rain until the school bus came along. The country roads left a lot to be desired, there was no pavement and very little gravel. Just plain old dirt roads. Mr. Ship was our school bus driver almost all the time I went to school. He was a great man and all the kids loved him. When the bus would get bogged down in the mud, all the boys would get out and push. Then when we arrived in school, we had mud all over us and it looked like we had been wallowing in a pig pen.

At six years old in the second grade, I was the youngest pupil in the class. That brought its own set of problems. Everyone in class was a year older than me. I had to fight with and compete with older kids all my years in the public schools. This really terrified me at first, but I finally adapted.

School was actually a lark. Arithmetic and reading were my favorite subjects. How wonderful that these two subjects are so practical in preparing a little barefoot boy for life. After school, Mother and Dad would see their son walking home down the muddy road with his arms loaded down with books. The only trouble was they never saw him studying them after he arrived home. After all, if you have spent a whole day in class, who wants to study and do homework after you get home. You have just got to take time to make pets out of that new litter of pigs, or see if you can ride that yearling calf without getting pitched off.

One thing I missed was having a horse to ride. We only had mules on our farm, and who wants to ride a mule? I decided that I would break some of our milk cows to ride. We had several that had sharp, wicked looking horns. I decided I would leave them alone and ride the ones that were muleys (no horns). So, with rope in hand, I would go out into the pasture to bring the cows in at milking time. After catching a cow and making a hackamore out of my rope, I would hop on board for the free ride home. Only the ride was not free. That old cow had her own idea about little boys hitching a free ride. Could she buck. Off I would go on my head or on my back. One time I was pitched into a clump of prickly pear. What I lacked in skill, I made up for in persistence. After bucking me off four or five times, the cow would give up and let me ride her home herding the other cows as we went. I would sit up there on that old milk cow and sing and yodel just like I imagined the real cowboys did.

One year, I broke a big yearling Hereford calf to ride. I took an old mule bridle and cut it down to size, leaving off the bit. Then in the mornings when I would go to round up the cattle and bring them to the pen, I would catch this yearling (a one year old) which I had taught to obey the reins, and we would drive the other cattle to the pens. One morning when I went to get the cattle, I found they were not to be found in the pasture but had broken through the barbwire fence and grazing in a field of green oats that was about knee high. I opened the gate from the field of oats to the pasture and went to catch my trusty steed. The yearling was a big pet and was very easy to catch. That morning I found out the meaning of the phrase "feeling your oats." Those old cows were feeling their oats that morning and were feeling frisky. When I got aboard my yearling and started to drive them, they all threw their tails up in the air and started for the corrals on the dead run. Of course, my yearling was right behind them.

Man, was I ever having fun. Sitting up there on that Hereford yearling, I could hear the wind whistling around my ears. That oat field was rushing by and I could imagine myself up on a real cow pony. When the cows came out of the oat field, they turned up the lane that led to the gate into the pasture. Fine, that was just what I wanted them to do. That is, they all turned but the yearling I was riding. The hole in the barbwire fence was a short cut to the corral, and the yearling went through that hole full steam ahead. The only problem was the boy sitting up on that yearling didn't fit and I was left plastered and tangled up in barbwire. That was my last time to ride the yearling. As far as I know, that homemade bridle rotted lying there at the hole in the fence.

4

Airplanes were my fascination during my growing up years. Dad could never get any work out of me when one was overhead. I would stand and watch it until it was completely out of sight. Luckily there were not many airplanes in those days. I made up my mind, someday I would be a pilot and fly one of those beautiful airplanes. Maybe I could even play tag with those white puffy clouds. What would it be like to just drag the wheels across the top of one of those clouds? The nearest airport was at Temple, Texas and was about 20 or 25 miles away. We only got that far from home about twice a year when my folks went to buy supplies. Once Dad took me to the airfield and there was a brand new yellow Piper Cub sitting in the hangar. I even got to look inside the airplane.

The Carters knew that if they wanted their little boy to grow up with the right attitudes and values, they had to instill those attitudes and values in him while he was still very young. My mother bought a Bible story book and spent hours reading the Bible stories to her son before he was old enough to read them himself. My father was both a Dad and a friend to his son. He would sit him astride the gasoline tank of the farm tractor and let him ride for hours while he plowed the fields. What high adventure for a six-year old. Best of all they taught him the values of loyalty, honesty, virtue, and good hard work; to set goals and then strive to attain them; to always give your best.

Church was something else in that part of the Texas farm country. It was still more than ten years before the historic meeting in the Texas Hotel when the Baptist Bible Fellowship would come into being. Previously there had been a Baptist church in the community, but because of the non-concern of the members, it had ceased to have services. Now it was a sad thing to see. Just an empty building, complete with pews, songbooks, and a piano but no preacher and no services. The only other church was a Methodist church about five miles away.

My folks were Baptists but they would rather go to a Methodist church than not to go to church at all. Dad and Mother would gather my sister and me into our old car and off we would go to church on Sundays. I learned that people are supposed to get saved, but it looked like to me that people who were Christians never had any fun. I decided that I would wait until I was about 80 years old and just about to die and then I would get saved. The way I had it figured out, I could live like the devil all my life and just before I died I would get saved and then I would not have to go to Hell for all eternity. Little boys may think a lot, but they don't always come up with the right answer.

Dad had me driving farm tractors and plowing cotton before my 12th birthday. Before that I would plow with the mules. It was a lot more fun driving the tractor. We would plow two rows at a time and then skip two rows. That way you didn't have to turn around so sharp at the end of the rows. I would plow two rows with one tractor and Dad would plow the next two rows with another tractor. If you worked it just right you could come to the end of the row, hit the power lift to raise the plows, spin the steering wheel and when the tractor was about half way around, hit the power lift again to drop the plows, and start plowing the other direction without ever slowing down. If you didn't do it just right, you plowed up a lot of cotton. Dad wasn't a killjoy, he knew that boys need to have a little fun.

Then I began to beg my Dad to let me drive the car. My argument was, if I could drive the tractors, why couldn't I drive the car? When I was about 13 years old, Dad started letting me drive the car around the farm. The trouble is that boys will try anything. One of the roads on the farm crossed a levee that was built to stop erosion. I had been in the habit of riding my bicycle at top speed, come up over that levee and making it fly through the air on the other side before it came to earth again. I thought, "If I can make the bicycle fly through the air, think how much further Dad's old '31 Chevy will fly." I wanted to wait for just the right time when no one was around to see me. Then, shades of Dukes of Hazard, here I came. I lined the old Chevy up, coming straight down that road right at the levee that stretched across the road. I went over the top and sure enough, it flew through the air just like my bicycle only it went a lot further. Something else, it came down a lot harder. There was a bone jarring jolt as it hit the ground, the hood flew up on both sides, and the sound was something else. It scared me so bad, I stopped to examine the damage. By pure luck, I hadn't destroyed Dad's car. I never did tell him what I did, but I wonder if he ever noticed all the new rattles.

Two things happened the summer I was fifteen. I met Harriett Taylor, the girl I would eventually marry, and a new preacher came into our community. I think I will tell about the new preacher first. He was really new, just four or five years older than me and he was a pastoral student at Baylor University in Waco, Texas, which was about 30 miles away. His name was James Lane and he was anxious to start a church while he was still in school. He went to the president of Baylor, Pat Neff, who was a former governor of Texas, and sought advice. Governor Neff's home farm was right there in our community and he knew there was no Baptist church for the people to go to. He sent him our way.

James Lane started visiting the farmers and asking them if they would be interested in helping to start a Baptist church. Dad was thrilled and promised him that if he would start one, the Carter family would attend. The first services were held in an open-air tabernacle at Mother Neff State Park. Pastor Lane would come on

Saturday and ask me to go visiting with him. I enjoyed it because he wasn't that much older than me and because I could ride in his 1937 Ford coupe. I thought that was really neat. I was not saved when we started visiting together, but it wasn't long until I began to be concerned. You see, Pastor Lane was not as much interested in having someone to visit with, as he was in seeing a country boy accept Christ as his Savior. One Sunday morning when the invitation was given, I stepped out of my seat and went to the front to accept Jesus Christ as my Savior. Then the new church took several of us down to a creek where we were baptized. I became one of the charter members of the Mother Neff Baptist Church.

That was the same summer of 1944 that I met my future bride, Harriett Ann Taylor. I did not know it at the time, but she was to become my life long companion, friend and sweetheart. I was not looking for a girlfriend, I already had one. I just went to Sidney, Texas, a very small place near Comanche, Texas to see my uncle, Charlie Carter and my cousins. But my cousin, Sally, had a close friend named Harriett. We met and after that trip I never had any other girlfriend but Harriett. We began to write to one another and although she lived over 100 miles away, occasionally I would get to go see her, riding a greyhound bus and carrying a guitar to serenade her. Her daddy had a shotgun and most of the boys were afraid to court her, but anybody that would jump a car over a levee shouldn't be afraid of a shotgun. I did walk pretty softly around there, but praise the Lord, her daddy liked me. Harriett thought I was very shy. I really was.

Moody High School graduated 35 students in the Spring of 1945 and I was still youngest in my class, just having turned 16 in January before graduation in May. My Uncle Charlie and his family came to my graduation from Sidney and brought Harriett with them. I got to show her off to my classmates at least that once.

It's hard to keep boys down on the farm. After I graduated, I was anxious to go out into the world and try to get a job. I would have liked to go to a business college but there was no money available. Times were hard on the farm. Dad asked me to stay until the crops were harvested and we would all move to town. He had a job as an electrician promised him. We moved to town that fall but Dad was sick and bedridden. He had what I now believe to have been rheumatic fever. Back then, everyone called it rheumatism. He had severe pain in his joints and had to be turned in bed with a sheet. I hired a truck to move us and we moved Dad right in his bed. He was laid up about eight months before he could work again.

I got a job as a route salesman for Pearcy's Fine Foods, a company that sold pies and potato chips. It was a very good job and paid as much in a day as you could make in a whole week working on the farm. The following year Harriett graduated from Sidney High School. I asked my boss for a few days off to go to her graduation and to get married. He thought I was crazy because Harriett and I were only 17 years old, but outside of getting saved, it was the smartest thing I ever did. I don't recommend it for anyone else, but it sure worked for us.

## Chapter 2  **THE FAMILY**

The next few years seemed to go quickly for the Barton Carter family. I had a variety of jobs, most of them involved in sales. When we were married, I was working for Pearcy's Foods selling direct to retail stores out of a cargo van. For a couple of years, I joined with my Dad in Carter and Son Electric. This was the time the rural electric companies were running electric lines out to the farming families who, up until then, had never had electricity. Our job was to wire existing houses that had never had electricity. It was much more challenging than installing wiring as the house was being built. We wired everything from ancient log houses to school houses.

My next job was working at the Bell Milk and Ice Cream Company. I did a little of everything there, but my main job was driving an ice cream truck on a rural route and selling ice cream to local retail grocery stores. From that job, I started work for Temple Feed and Fuel selling feed and grain for farm animals to feed stores in 26 counties in central Texas. I worked out of an automobile and sold as many as five semi-trucks of feed a day plus sometimes a freight train carload. I was paid a $2 bonus when I sold a carload.

Our church attendance suffered after we were married. When Harriett and I would go to the local Baptist church, they would not take into consideration that we were married, but would send us to classes arranged by age and sex. Harriett generally wound up with teenage girls and I would end up with teenage boys. We just did not fit in, the members were not very friendly, and we quit going and no one from church even visited.

During this time our first two children were born, Gloria Ann in 1947 and Sandra Kay in 1948. Photography was my hobby and I took many pictures of my sweet little girls. I set up a darkroom and developed my own pictures and dealt mostly in black and white.

Then we decided to relocate from Temple, Texas to El Paso, Texas. An uncle who lived in El Paso convinced me that there were many more opportunities for young men in El Paso than in Temple. We made the move and I continued to work in sales, selling grocery specialties to retail stores up and down the Rio Grande valley. Next, I went to work for Safeway Stores, becoming a checker, stocker, and then head produce clerk in the days just before the supermarket era. After working outside my entire life, I hated being cooped up all day long in one place. I was able to transfer to the trucking department where I drove a semi-truck and delivered groceries, produce, and meat to the Safeway stores in New Mexico and west Texas.

While working at Safeway Stores, our next two children were born, Kathy Sue in 1952 and Michael Barton in 1955. While in El Paso, I began to realize my dream to become a pilot. I enrolled in pilot training and soloed in a J3 Piper Cub at El Paso International Airport in 1949.

A friend who was driving for Navajo Freight Lines in Albuquerque, New Mexico challenged me to come apply with them as the wages were about double what I was making at Safeway. I applied, was hired, and moved my family to Albuquerque. At Navajo Freight lines, my job was driving a truck with two drivers and a sleeper cab. One would drive while the other slept. A trip generally ran from 60 to 72 hours and then I would be off for about 36 hours. Lots of time to be with family and to have family outings. It involved lots of miles. My driving partner and I took possession of a new truck in 1958 and by 1962 we had put one million miles on it.

It was a good move in many ways, mainly because Harriett found a good church we could worship in. It was Berean Baptist Church and was an independent church affiliated with Baptist Bible Fellowship. With a good income, we were able to purchase our first home and I bought my first airplane, a 1948 Cessna 170. I used this airplane to get both my private and my commercial pilot license. I sold this airplane to Bobby Unser, who would become famous as an Indy race driver. I also flew with his brother, Indy race driver, Al Unser.

One of our greatest family times was camping trip vacations. A tent that folded into a trailer, a Coleman stove and lantern was all we needed to have a great vacation. As Harriett cooked for the family all the time, I insisted on doing all the cooking while we were camping out. We toured Grand Canyon National Park, Yellowstone National Park, Oak Creek Canyon and the Painted Desert in Arizona, and Mesa Verde in Colorado plus many other points of interest.

I then bought a 1950 Beechcraft Bonanza, a beautiful red and white, trimmed in black airplane with retractable gear and controllable prop. We would use it to visit family in Dallas or El Paso where my parents and sister lived. My folks had relocated from Temple to El Paso a few years after we did.

Our church was becoming very important in our lives. Our children were saved there, and several surrendered their lives to the Lord. Our oldest daughter, Gloria, graduated from high school and went to Springfield, Missouri to attend Baptist Bible College where she met and eventually married Lowell Haggerty who later pastored churches in Missouri and Ohio. Sandra attended Baptist Bible College for a time and Kathy graduated from there along with her husband, Larry Bice.

Berean Baptist Church was growing rapidly, and we were bursting at the seams. Pastor Yates led the church in buying new property to build a bigger church building. The way of financing it was by interest bearing church bonds. The bonds were then sold for cash to church members and anyone who wanted to make an investment. One night, driving my truck to Chicago, God began to speak to my heart about buying some of the church bonds. I was surprised, and I answered, "God, I don't have any money to invest in church bonds." He answered, "You have got an airplane you can sell, and then you can buy church bonds."

When I returned home, I told Harriett that I was going to sell our airplane and buy church bonds. She was very surprised as she knew how much I liked to fly that airplane. But I was learning a valuable lesson, to trust God when He told me to do something. God knew that in a few years He had something for me to do and those church bonds would finance a lot of things, money I would use over and over again.

A couple of years later God began dealing with me in a different way. When attending church, I would feel like I should go forward when the invitation was given. I rejected this feeling because I knew that I was already saved. What did I need to go forward for? But the feeling just became more intense until finally I spoke to Pastor Charlie Yates about it in his office. His reply, "Bart, God is trying to talk to you and you are not listening."

On the way back to the auditorium I started listening. I could only hear God speak one word, "surrender." The thought scared me to death. How could I surrender? Too many people were depending on me. I would have to give up my job. How could I provide for my family? I didn't even know what God wanted me to do. I felt I needed time to think about this.

When I went into the auditorium I breathed a sigh of relief, we had a missionary, Rev. Lavern Rogers, speaking that evening. I thought, he is a missionary, he will tell about his field and he will not preach, and I can have more time to think about surrendering. He did tell about his field, but he also preached, and God was working on my heart. Then he extended the invitation. Our song leader almost always used the song, "Just as I Am" for the invitational, but that night as the Lord was urging me to surrender, the song leader used the song, "I Surrender All." I could not wait any longer, I almost ran to the altar. The associate pastor knelt with me and asked, "Bart, what did you come for?" I told him, "I came to surrender." He then asked, "What did you come to surrender for?" I answered, "I do not know, I am surrendering for anything God wants me to do." He asked "What if God wants you to be a missionary? Are you willing to do that?" I had not even thought about being a missionary, but I answered, "If that's what God wants me to do, then I will do it."

That night, I surrendered my life to the Lord and had no idea what God wanted me to do. That same night, just after midnight, I was dispatched to drive a load of freight to Oakland, California. About daylight as I was nearing Gallup, New Mexico I began to think of the decision I had made earlier that evening. God knew what He wanted me to do, if I wanted to know what it was, all I had to do was to ask Him. As I was driving a heavily loaded freight truck, I began to pray and ask God what He wanted me to do. God's answer was not in an audible voice, but He spoke to my heart as plain as if it had been in an audible voice. God told me He wanted me to be a missionary in the Philippine Islands. From that moment forward I never doubted my call, or that I had to prepare myself to fulfill that call. Later that day from Fresno, California I called Harriett and told her that God wanted us to be missionaries in the

Philippine Islands. She told me she was willing to go with me anywhere God called us. This in spite of the fact that she had told me before we married that she did not want to live on an island.

On Wednesday when we returned to Albuquerque at the end of our trip I began to burn my bridges behind me. I told my bosses at Navajo Freight Lines that God had called me to be a missionary and that I would be leaving my job the coming summer and moving to Springfield, Missouri to attend Baptist Bible College. It was November 1966 when God called me to surrender and I wanted to enroll in the fall of 1967 at the Bible College.

That evening at the Wednesday night service, Pastor Yates asked me, "Bart, what does God want you to do?" He knew that God would have revealed it to me by then. When I related that God wanted me to be a missionary in the Philippines his answer was, "Bart, you are too old to be a missionary." I told him that I knew nothing of what the requirements were but that I was certain what God wanted with me. He said, "Okay then, if you are going to be a missionary, you preach this Sunday evening service." I made another trip before Sunday and preached my first sermon ever in November 1966.

We then started preparations to move to Springfield. We had to eliminate any debt, downsize our car, sell things we could not take with us, and put our house on the market to sell. Rev. Jack Haggerty had a house and ½ acre of land just a half mile from the Baptist Bible College. He was asking $3,000 and he was willing to take $3,000 of those church bonds I had bought in lieu of cash. I now had a place to live while in college and when I graduated, I sold it for $5,000. God can do a much better job of managing your finances than you.

## Chapter 3 – **Bible College**

Twenty-two years after I graduated from high school, I moved to Springfield, Missouri to enroll in Baptist Bible College. Our two oldest daughters were already married leaving the two youngest still home. Because of our calling as missionaries, Harriett had to enroll as a full-time student also. Both are missionaries, both must be trained.

Finding a job with hours where I could both earn a living and still go to school full-time was difficult. As a Bible college student, every time you go to work you are representing Jesus Christ. You try to be the best worker on the job. I made a living working for different freight companies, loading and unloading trucks and delivering or picking up freight around Springfield.

Finding a new church to attend was first on our to-do list. Our pastor had told us not to be "church tramps" but find the church God wanted us in and then stay there. Our oldest daughter, Gloria, and her husband, Lowell Haggerty, went to High Street Baptist Church, so we went there first. God spoke to our hearts and that's where we attended all through Bible school. I drove one of the church busses and taught Sunday School classes plus taught at Daily Vacation Bible School. Dr. David Cavin was our pastor and a great man. He and High Street Baptist Church licensed me to preach the Gospel.

We enrolled in Bible college in the mission course that would be carefully crafted to groom us in what we would need to know to be missionaries, similar but slightly different from the pastor course. After 22 years since high school, we had to learn to study all over again.

That included setting goals and budgeting our time. Both would prove to be invaluable over all our years as missionaries as well as in college. Our professors all taught from an outline and a friend taught me how to study for my tests with that outline. I could anticipate every question the professor could ask and then answer the questions. Seldom was a question on a test that I hadn't anticipated. There were certain professors that quickly became favorites. On registration mornings, Harriett and I would get in line before sunrise so that we could be near the front of the line to get the professors we wanted. All the professors were tremendous and had proven themselves in the churches before they became professors.

Rev. Jack Bridges was our mission professor. His three-year outline was, "the man, the method, and the message." On one of our first days of class, he taught about the requirements to be an approved missionary. He told the class to come to him after class if we did not meet the requirements. Rev. Yates had been correct, I was too old to be a missionary. I stayed after class and talked to Brother Bridges. I told him I did not meet the age requirements but there was no way I could turn back my age. He and I then met with Doctor Donnelson, the mission director of Baptist Bible Fellowship International. After questioning me about my call, whether my wife was attending, and my course of study, he told me that Baptist Bible Fellowship might not be able to approve me as a Fellowship missionary. My answer was that Baptist Bible Fellowship had not been called to send me to the Philippines, but that God had called me to the Philippines. Therefore, it was my job to get to the Philippines. He seemed pleased with that answer and told me to continue my studies and see what God would do.

It was during Bible college that I became aware of the faith promise offering. Our church in Albuquerque had practiced giving 10% of its total income for missions. Faith Promise was so much better, and it was right there in the Bible how to do it. We started out with just a couple of dollars a week and it was amazing how God would almost miraculously supply. As our faith increased year by year so did our faith promise offering increase. When God finds that He can trust you to channel the money where He wants it, He begins to send more and more through you.

College was so important to Harriett and me, that we vowed to never miss a day in all our years at Bible college. By God's grace we were able to keep that vow. During the graduation ceremonies, Professor Eli Harju made a special announcement that Barton and Harriett Carter had never missed a day or even been tardy the entire time we attended Baptist Bible College. Then he said, "May their tribe increase."

College was also a time for making life-long friends, friends that would one day be pastoring churches and supporting the Carters as they labored on the mission field. In high school I was the youngest in the class. In college Harriett and I were a generation older than almost everyone else. In fact, while still freshmen, Harriett and I became grandparents. Catherine Haggerty was born December 31, 1967. Our fellow classmates began to call us "gramps" and "granny." By graduation Renee Edwards and Denise Haggerty were born and we had three grandchildren.

One important thing to learn is that college is not just to teach you things, but to teach you how to study things on your own. If you don't learn how to study, you run out of material after a few years. If you learn how to apply yourself, you will have material for a life time. A missionary is constantly teaching others the lessons he has been taught and teaching others to study things on their own. The great commission states, *"Go ye therefore, and teach all nations, baptizing them in the name of the Father, and of the Son, and of the Holy Ghost: Teaching them to observe all things whatsoever I have commanded you, and lo, I am with you alway, even unto the end of the world. Amen."* Matthew 28:19-20.

During my Senior year at Baptist Bible College, I met two missionaries from the Philippines. Brother Bob Hughes and Brother Damon Woods were both on furlough, and both challenged me to come to their areas to work. Brother Woods had an airplane and wanted me to come to Baguio City to work and to fly his airplane for him. Brother Hughes just wanted more Bible college teachers and more church planters in Cebu City. Even though the airplane ministry was intriguing, when I prayed for God's direction I was told to go to Cebu City. Now I knew exactly where God wanted me to minister in the Philippines.

## Chapter 4 – **Internship and Deputation**

After graduation, Pastor Charlie Yates of Berean Baptist Church in Albuquerque, the church we had been in before college, asked us to come back for our required one-year internship. We moved back to Albuquerque into a house that Berean had for its workers.

In college, the professors were teaching us knowledge. When you are an intern, you must learn wisdom. Wisdom is the proper application of knowledge. There is a big difference between learning and doing. In the church is where the rubber meets the road. Pastor Yates taught me how to work. We kept a log sheet and made 25 to 30 visits a day on follow up. Plus, sometimes we did census work and visited house to house where we would make a hundred calls a day. Berean had a reputation as a soul-winning church, and we tried to see that folks at least got to hear the Gospel. During my year of internship God used me to lead 67 people to Him for salvation.

While we had been in college, Berean had grown by leaps and bounds. They had a fleet of busses that brought children in from all around our section of Albuquerque. A second story had been built on the Sunday School section, but the auditorium could only handle about 300 to 350. To handle the 800 or more that attended, they had to be preached to where they attended Sunday School. I was made the Junior High Pastor. There were ten junior high classes with individual teachers, a junior high song leader and a junior high pianist. After Sunday School, we had a regular worship service with just junior highs and their teachers. I would preach just to the junior highs. This was where I actually learned how to read an audience and to preach. If their attention started to waver, I would do something different to get their attention back. Sometimes I might run up and down the aisle or to act out what I was preaching. I was also able to focus my message on things that mattered to this age group. A normal Sunday would have about 120 to 125 in the junior high audience and anywhere from five to ten saved. The entire church averaged about 40 to 50 salvations each week.

Berean had built the Singing Hills Youth Camp just before we went to Bible college. Each summer churches from all over Texas, Colorado, and New Mexico sent their kids there for youth camp. Berean had bought several retired Greyhound buses to help transport these children to and from youth camp. As a former truck driver, I was used to drive one of those buses. It was at the Singing Hills Youth Camp where many of the West Texas and New Mexico pastors were gathered, that I was ordained as a Baptist preacher.

After the 1970 Christmas vacation, Pastor Yates offered to allow all the New Mexico Bible college students a ride back to Springfield on one of our diesel busses. I drove the bus and Harriett accompanied me for the trip to Springfield and back. When returning home, on the freeway between Springfield and Joplin, I asked Harriett to drive as I wanted to check out the seating in different places while the bus was in motion. There were very few women driving big rigs at that time. A pickup truck passed with three men inside. They looked up as they passed and saw a woman driving that big bus. They were so shocked Harriett said they were looking out the back window of that pickup until they went out of sight.

The first time I ever heard someone get saved in another language was at the youth camp. I was one of the workers at the front when the invitation was given, and a Navajo Indian young person came to get saved. The Navajo pastor led him to the Lord in the Navajo language. I almost came unglued, to think that my God can respond to any language anywhere in the world is mind boggling. If that won't get you excited nothing will.

As my year of internship was winding down, I began making plans to start deputation. I wrote a letter to Dr. David Cavin telling him of my plans and he answered that High Street Baptist Church wanted to be the first church to support me with a $50 monthly offering. That eventually grew to $100 a month and has not missed a month in the last 46 years.

Another response came from Dr. Philips, missionary to the Navajo Indians. He told me that I should start my deputation on the mission field and asked me to come preach for him as he was going to be away from his pulpit. His Navajo preacher would be there and would be my interpreter. When I first arrived, the Navajo pastor was out bringing people in to church. Older Navajos were the only ones in the church at the time and we could not communicate. They were probably wondering who is this white man?

Later the Navajo pastor returned, and we planned the service. I would speak to the young people class in Sunday School as they could all speak English. During worship service I would preach, and he would interpret. Heaven came down that morning. When the invitation was given, Navajos streamed forward. People were at the altar praying aloud in the Navajo language. There were more that came than there were workers. The pastor who had been leading the invitation song had to go to work the altar himself. He told me to lead the singing. They were singing in Navajo, but the tune was still the same, so I just sang in English as they were singing in Navajo. If I remember correctly, there were ten saved that morning.

When service was over, I was asked to stand in the foyer and shake hands with the people. One of the young people stood by me and interpreted. Many of the older people brought paper and wanted me to write my name and address. Later, when I saw Dr. Philips again, I asked about this. He said, "Brother Carter, most of those people cannot read what you wrote, but they will look at that paper and remember you and pray for you." Praise the Lord!

The lean financial times started when we left the employ of Berean Baptist and started deputation full-time. Missionary Bob Hughes had given me some slides of the Philippines and taught me how to present our needs while showing them. We lived off the love offerings the churches gave me when I would preach for them while presenting the mission field of the Philippine Islands. There is a several months delay after you preach in a church, and they vote to support you, before you start getting the monthly support. In 1971, the average church would give a $25 honorarium and the average monthly support was $15. We put our faith in the Lord and somehow, He always saw us through.

To be more centrally located, we moved back to Springfield, Missouri and bought a mobile home that belonged to Ron Roach who had just graduated from Bible college and was starting a new church, Great Falls Baptist Temple in Great Falls, Montana. Again, I used Berean Baptist church bonds to buy the mobile home. Again, I rejoiced that I had listened when God told me to sell the airplane and buy church bonds. God had been taking care of us all the time! When we finished deputation, and sold the mobile home, we used the money again to buy a printing press and a print shop camera to make printing plates to print tracts and lessons in the Philippines. Our son, Mike, wanted to serve as our printer and had taken a trade school course in printing in high school. He was taught to fill any position, or job to be done in a print shop.

Rev. Jack Bridges was now mission director of the BBFI, and he thought there was a way for several who wanted to be approved but were over the age limit or disqualified for some reason or other, to be approved. We went up for approval at the national fellowship meeting in Abilene, Texas. We were approved by the mission committee, but the directors of the Fellowship vetoed all the ones who had applied. It was a disheartening moment. Harriett and I went back to our motel room. I told her, "If I was a quitter, now would be the time to quit, but I am not a quitter." We knelt by the bed and began to pray for God's guidance. I went back to the fellowship meeting, sought out Dr. David Cavin and asked if High Street Baptist Church would be both my sending church and my mission office. Upon his approval, I took out my appointment book and began to make appointments to go to churches to present our need to get to the Philippine Islands. My problem was, I could not present myself as a Fellowship missionary, so I had to go mostly to people who knew me or knew of me. Here is where my classmates from the class of '70 came in. Many were already pastoring churches and many of them were willing to support us.

Our class mates were scattered all over the United States. That caused us to drive over 70,000 miles in the year we spent on deputation. God blessed, almost 200 souls were saved, and 33 had surrendered their lives for full-time service. We then started planning for our departure for the Philippines. We applied for visas from the Philippine government several months ahead of our departure date as we had been instructed. We booked passage on States Line freighter S.S. Hawaii bound for the Philippines. Brother David Hardy helped me crate my belongings and he and his 10-year old son, Wayne, went with me to Kansas City where we shipped them to Roy Hendrickson of Fellowship Packing and Crating via Navajo Freight Lines, the same company I had worked for.

On the way to California, we stopped to preach at Berean Baptist Church in Albuquerque, New Mexico. This was the church we had been called from. We were still lacking $3,000 having enough money to pay for our shipping and passage. That evening, Brother Yates told the church our need and they raised the $3,000 that night.

In Los Angeles, we got all our immunizations that were required, we had our passports, but the Philippine visas had still not come in. As the day drew nearer we had to make a decision. Our baggage was to be loaded at L.A., but we were to board the ship a week later in San Francisco. Should we load the baggage on faith and hope our visas got to us in time? We prayed, and loaded the baggage. Just before going to San Francisco, we checked the embassy one last time for our visas. It was not there. The embassy suggested giving us a visitor's visa that was good for 59 days, and they would direct our visas to be delivered to Hong Kong which was on the ship's itinerary. We accepted the visitor's visa and left to board the ship in San Francisco.

# Chapter 5 – **Philippine Islands**

Going to the Philippines by ship was a wise decision. We were allowed a lot more carry-on baggage, we rested for almost a month, and we built up an extra month's support. But there was a problem. A typhoon had caused the ship to not be able to take the shortest route to Hong Kong where we were to pick up our visas. The Captain told me we would arrive in Hong Kong Friday evening and leave before Monday morning. I was able to get the radio officer to use the ship-to-shore radio to contact the telephone system in Hong Kong to dial the Philippine Embassy. They confirmed they were closed on Saturday but told me to knock on the door and they would let us in to pick up our visas.

Saturday morning, the three of us went ashore and took a taxi to the Philippine Embassy. When we knocked on the door they let us enter. But the news was not good. I was told that since I had called, they had searched for our visas, but they were not there. I then asked if we could pick up our visas in Manila and was told visas could not be picked up in the Philippines but had to be picked up out of the country. We would have to come back to Hong Kong after our visas arrived there. We could still enter the Philippines with our visitor's visa. I then asked if Harriett and Mike could sign for their visas so that only one of us would have the expense of returning to Hong Kong. The answer was we would all three have to return. We were heartbroken and did not pay much attention when a man entered the office and handed the embassy official an envelope. He opened the envelope, glanced inside, and then asked me to tell him my full name again. When I answered, he said, "What do you know, I have just been handed your visas." There were three happy missionaries with tears in their eyes standing in that office. If there had been no typhoon we would have arrived on Friday and the visas would not have been there. God had been testing our faith and also teaching us that we could always trust Him. God had delayed our ship until the visas could be obtained.

A couple days later, we sailed past Corregidor and into Manila Bay. Standing on the dock to meet us were missionaries Bob and Helen Hughes and Bill and Dorothy Merritt. They made our entry so much easier because they were right at home in the Philippines and knew just what we had to do. I preached my first sermon in the Philippines in the church pastored by Brother Merritt.

When we were about half-way across the Pacific Ocean on our way to the Philippines, President Marcos declared martial law. One of the sailors on our ship, a Filipino, heard about it on short wave radio and told us. We were very concerned at the time, but it helped immensely when checking through customs. The customs officials were afraid to make us pay bribes. We reshipped our supplies via inter-island shipping to Cebu City where we intended to go to language school and start our ministry teaching in the Bible Baptist College of Cebu City.

We flew into Cebu and were met at the airport by the Bible Baptist Church of Cebu City that was pioneered by Missionary Bob Hughes. They were holding a huge banner welcoming the Carters to the Philippines. The airport was an old American air base on a separate island from Cebu. We were shuttled to Cebu Island on an old landing craft from World War II. A few years later, a bridge was built, and the landing craft were retired.

Missionary John Honeycutt opened his home to the Carters until we found a house that we could rent. We found a house in a fenced compound. The house had five bedrooms and two baths. It was a large house but we used one bedroom for the print shop, it's walk-in closet for the dark room, another bedroom for my office and study, our bedroom, Mike's bedroom, and the guest room. It was sure a mess when we rented it. Three or four families had been living in it, and it was sure dirty. We had it plumbed for hot water, gas lines put in for the stove, hot water heater and propane clothes dryer, and painted it inside and out. We wanted all the walls and ceilings painted off-white. The Filipino painter was used to painting different rooms different colors and he had a problem understanding. He kept saying, "You want everything off-white?" I told him, "Yes, I want everything off-white." The problem was, the living room had a beautifully paneled wood wall. You guessed it, when I returned the paneled wall was painted off-white. Harriett opened one of the kitchen cabinet drawers and found they had painted right over a lizard that was in the drawer. She had to scrape up the dead lizard and repaint where he had been. The back yard was an eyesore, so we poured concrete on part of it and built a wash house and storehouse combined. The rent was about $64.75 when converted from pesos to dollars.

A great many people spoke English, but communication was still a problem. They sure didn't speak or understand Texan. I told the plumber I wanted hot water to the shower and lavatory. The next time I looked, he had two shower heads in the shower, one for the hot water and one for the cold water, just like the lavatory. He had never taken a hot shower in his life and didn't realize you had to mix the water or you would scald on one side and freeze on the other. The pipes were running everywhere. Then the gas man came to hook up the gas and we found the plumber had hooked the cold-water pipes to the hot-water outlet on the water heater, and the hot-water pipes to the cold-water inlet. We would have been flushing the toilet with hot water.

We had to get used to the different noises. We slept with the windows open, and about 4:30 in the morning the roosters would start to crow, and pigs would squeal, and the Filipinos began to get up and start stirring around. There were enough roosters around that there was one crowing all the time. The first night we were in our house we lay there for about 30 minutes to an hour after the crowing began. Then Harriett got up and began to flap her arms and crow like a rooster. I knew it was time to get up.

Temple Baptist Church of Detroit sent a crate of Bibles to Bob Hughes to be included with our shipment of crates. Brother Hughes placed the Bibles in the song book racks along with the song books. They were to be used at church and not taken home. Then he asked for everyone to pick up one of the Bibles. Then he said, "If this is the first time you have ever held a Bible, hold up your hand." About a hundred hands went up. What a shocker. It was eye-opening for me. A hundred people that were in church, not only did not own a Bible, but had never before even touched one before.

One Sunday evening, Missionary Bob Hughes asked me to preach at Bible Baptist Church of Cebu City. I used Mark, chapter five for a text, and preached about the wild man of the Gadarenes that no man could bind. The demons that were possessing the man recognized Jesus as the Son of God, and begged Him not to torment them. They begged not to be sent out of the country but to be allowed to enter the herd of swine that was near. When I got to the point in my sermon where the swine were running into the sea, pigs started squealing all around the church! The church was right in town and I did not know there were pigs even there. The squealing almost drowned out my preaching. Then a woman in the audience jumped up out of her seat and started pointing at me and shouting in a man's voice! I had preached up a demon! Two of the deacons came and escorted the woman out of the church. The next day Brother Hughes dealt with her personally.

Mrs. Jesalva, the pastor's wife became our language teacher, we set up a room in the church for the three missionary family's children to take their correspondence courses, and I began to teach at the Bible college. Mike stayed busy with the printing press printing tracts, the church paper, and even a Cebuano language songbook. Our learning process had begun, and I was teaching some students that would eventually pastor some of the churches I helped them start.

In the fall of 1972, the only independent Baptist church on the Island of Negros was at San Isidro. They were having an anniversary service, and they contacted Dr. Jesalva and asked for several of our preachers to attend. Dr. Jesalva promised them he would send me along. My trip to San Isidro was eye opening. It was my first trip way out in the province, and the anniversary lasted several days. It had been so long since they had seen an American, the children, at first, were afraid of me. The Filipinos are short, and I looked like a giant to them. When I preached, the church would be packed with adults and all the windows would have children looking in. It was there God called Jun Villaflor into full-time service, the first to surrender under my preaching in the Philippines. Forty-five years later, he is still pastoring a church.

Returning from the anniversary service, we rode a bus into San Carlos City, a city with a population of 126,000. The bus terminal was at the edge of town and we rode pedicabs (bicycle with a side car used as taxis) to the downtown area. It was just getting daylight and I was riding with Filipino pastor Jess Enod. The Lord began speaking to my heart, "This is the town I want you to start a church." I told Brother Enod, "God is talking to me right now to build a church in this place." He answered, "Praise the Lord, we have been praying for someone to come to this town."

Pastor Hughes wanted to visit Fedalina and Thelma Mahilum, sisters who had been saved in Cebu City. When we knocked on their door and they opened the door, instead of inviting us in, they just burst out in tears and Fedalina said, "Praise the Lord, we have been praying for someone to come to San Carlos City." She didn't know that only 15 minutes before, God had called me to build a church in San Carlos. It may be that God's directing me to the Philippines in the first place was an answer to her prayer. God is omniscient and knew she would be praying for San Carlos long before she prayed the prayer.

We planned a first service for the new work for January 14, 1973. Because of the great need for Bibles, Missionary Bob Hughes had begun printing New Testaments. By using newsprint paper, he could have them printed for about 10 cents each. Mike began to print up invitations to come to the first service, and we promised everyone who came, they would get a Bible. The local radio station gave us free announcements of the opening service. The Mahilum sisters had a large living room and we were going to use that temporarily.

On January 13th, I caught the ferry boat from Cebu island to Negros. Accompanying me was Jun Villaflor who was an accordion player, and a student from the Bible college who would be song leader. On the ferry boat between the islands, I had been witnessing to a Filipino man. Just as we entered the San Carlos harbor, he accepted Jesus as his Savior and was my first convert in San Carlos. We passed out gospel tracts, conducted several services in outlying barrios and on Sunday morning had an attendance of 178 for our very first service. Total saved for the two-day period was a total of

44 souls. We started the new mission in San Carlos under the authority of the Bible Baptist Church of Cebu City and they voted us the authority to baptize. The next Saturday, we baptized 19 of the 44 in the Pacific Ocean. For the first four weeks our average attendance was 119, with 117 saved, 29 baptized, and another baptismal service planned. Rev. David Hardy wrote and said, "Now let someone try to tell me that Grandpa Carter is too old to be a missionary."

On the 27th of January, the Mahilum family invited me and my two co-workers to have lunch with them. They sat me at the head of the table because they said I was the privileged guest. It was typical Filipino food of chicken, fish, rice, etc. Each person had a bowl of chicken and cabbage soup. A cabbage leaf was floating on the top of my soup and when I ate the cabbage I found a chicken head floating in my soup: eyes, bill, comb and all. I really didn't know how to eat a chicken head, so I just ate the comb. It was pretty good. When I asked Mrs. Jesalva, my language teacher, about it, she told me that I got the head because I was the privileged guest. She said when she was growing up all the children wanted the head.

About one month after the start-up of Bible Baptist Mission of San Carlos, Brother Juanito Vale became our associate pastor. He was to visit full time and would hold the mid-week services. He had been the associate pastor at San Isidro where we had gone for the anniversary service back in November. He was a graduate of Bible Baptist College of Cebu City and had been active in the work for several years. He was married and had two little daughters. The smallest one was scared of Harriett because of her lighter skin and thought she might be a ghost. She would cry when Harriett tried to talk to her. I told her, "Do not worry little girl, I cried the first time I saw her also."

We rented a store front building right on the plaza, had pews made by local carpenters, and started a bus ministry using motorcabs (small motorcycles with sidecars) to bring in folks from the barrios. A small 100 to 150 cc motorcab could haul 10 to 14 people. There was no electricity in San Carlos. We used kerosene or propane lanterns for the evening services. Then everyone walked home in the dark. Most of the time when someone got saved we baptized them that day, if it was a daylight service. I heard that the San Carlos people had a saying, "If you go to that Baptist church, you are going to come home wet."

I performed my first wedding in the Philippines on the 17<sup>th</sup> of March at San Isidro on the island of Negros. When I was asked to perform the marriage ceremony, I asked, "Is it going to be a big wedding?" I was trying to find out if people were going to be marching down the aisle and things like that. They answered, "Yes they are going to kill a *baca* (beef) instead of a pig."

The time of the wedding was to be at 10am on a Saturday, so I had to come on Friday evening in order to have a rehearsal. I left Cebu City at noon Friday and it was about an hour after dark when I and the people from the church at San Carlos got off the bus at the closest bus stop to San Isidro. Some of the San Carlos members were going to participate in the wedding. The pastor of the San Isidro church was there at the bus stop waiting for us. We waited until an old six by six army truck (W.W. II vintage) pulled up, and we all climbed up in the truck bed and rode up the mountain to San Isidro. When we arrived, most of the guests were already there and had butchered the beef. This was all taking place at the groom's parents' house. The first thing they wanted us to do was eat, and they had plenty of food. After eating, we went outside where the great majority of people were, and the outside was lighted up with kerosene lanterns. These kerosene lanterns give just as much light as a Coleman gasoline lantern but they operate on kerosene instead of gasoline.

Then they decided that they would have an evangelistic service. They sang for a while in Cebuano. I had brought the accordion for the wedding the next day, and I also brought my accordion player and song leader. The Filipino pastor was reading his Bible to the crowd, so I thought he was going to preach. I was sitting on a log very tired out when I heard the pastor introduce me in the dialect. I leaned over to my accordion player and asked, "What did he just say?" He said, "You are going to be the one to preach, Pastor." So, I opened my Bible and got up and preached. That was the shortest notice I ever had that I was going to be the speaker.

After the service was over that night, it was a little after 10pm, and we still had to have the rehearsal. Everyone who was in the wedding went down to the church to go through the motions and a lot of others just went along to watch. The Filipino wedding is a lot like a Stateside wedding except more people are involved. There were three groomsmen besides the groom and best man. Then there was the bride, the maid of honor, and three bridesmaids. Then there were two little girls and one little boy. One of the little girls was the flower girl, the little boy was the ringbearer, and I never found out what the other little girl was for. Then besides all those, there were four sponsors for the groom and four sponsors for the bride. I had fun trying to show everyone what to do when several of them did not understand English. When the rehearsal was over, it was 15 minutes past midnight.

The next morning the church had been decorated with crepe paper and a runner down the aisle. It really looked nice. When the wedding started everyone really looked nice. All the girls in the wedding party had on evening dresses although none of them matched. The groom and best man had on suits and ties, but the other three groomsmen had on dark pants and white shirts but no ties. I wore my *barong*, which is a fancy Filipino shirt that is used for formal occasions.

After all the vows and questions, I pronounced them husband and wife, and when I told him he could kiss his bride; he just stood there. Everyone was prompting him and saying, "kiss, kiss, kiss." Finally, he understood and he carefully lifted her veil back over her head and off her face. Then instead of kissing her, they touched foreheads. He was too embarrassed to kiss her in front of an audience. I had a hard time to keep from laughing.

In San Carlos City, the man we rented our storefront from was owner of the local radio station. We were able to buy 15 minutes of radio time per week at a cost of about $2 per session. Preaching on the radio reached some of the outlying towns, and one group started coming by bus to our services from Calatrava, a town about 15 kilometers away. Then they started bringing visitors and the visitors were getting saved and baptized. Eventually we had 30 baptized members in Calatrava. God spoke to my heart to start a church in Calatrava so they could have a church in their own town. That church is still alive and well as I am writing this book.

As our church was right on the plaza, our joyful singing attracted lots of attention. Sometimes there would be as many as 50 people standing outside listening to the singing. Sunday was market day with people from out of town there to buy supplies. One Sunday a man came in, listened to the gospel, and responded when the invitation was given. After accepting the Lord as his Savior, he was baptized along with the others being baptized that day. Brother Vale told me he was from Camaniangan, a community that was a five hour walk up in the mountains. There were no roads there. The only way to get there was to walk. I was happy he had been saved but did not expect to ever see him again. Imagine my surprise when the next Sunday he was back and had brought visitors with him. When the invitation was given he brought his visitors to the altar for salvation.

As our services started at 8:30 AM, these Camaniangan people had to leave about noon on Saturday to come to church. They would stay overnight at a community on the outskirts of San Carlos with a name that when translated into English meant "Breakfast." Then it would take all of Sunday afternoon for them to get back home. Think about how much these folks wanted to go to church to expend that much effort. A trip to church took 36 hours!

Week after week turned into month after month. The gentleman kept bringing his friends and neighbors to be saved and baptized. God again spoke to my heart, "These people need a church in their community." We had baptized about 25 folks from that community and that became the core for a new church.

To organize the church, I, Brother Vale, and Brother Bensing, another of our elders made the five-hour hike up the mountain. The day before our trip, Brother Vale asked me what shoes I was going to wear. I had on a pair of Sears dress shoes so I told him that I would wear them. He said, "I don't think that will work, we will be crossing a river." I said, "I will pull them off, wade across and then put them back on." Again, he said, "I don't think that will work." I had been in the Philippines long enough to know that if he didn't think it would work, it definitely would not work. I went to the market to look for some tennis shoes. It was the only time in the Philippines that I found a pair of shoes big enough to fit me. On the trip into the mountains, I found out why the dress shoes would not work. The trail followed a stream flowing out of the mountains.

The trail crossed the small river 50 times before we got there. We were wading in water so much our feet were always wet.

Upon arrival, we met a 79-year-old grandmother who was blind. She would never have been able to hike that trail out of the mountains. Brother Vale witnessed to her and she was saved. I baptized her the next day in that mountain river. She had never seen a baptism and was very surprised when I put her under the water.

After we arrived, the women made coffee for us and began to prepare lunch. They served the coffee with cream and sugar. Someone had brought the sugar all the way from San Carlos. The only trouble was, sugar ants had gotten into the sugar. Those ants were floating on the top of my coffee. I took a spoon and was taking them out when Brother Vale said, "Brother Carter, those ants will not hurt you, they are dead already." I picked them out anyway, but that evening when it was dark, they served me coffee again. I could taste the sugar in the coffee and I knew the ants were floating there but I could not see them. Brother Vale was right. The ants did not hurt me.

When all the men met to discuss building a church, different ones donated different things for the church. One man offered property for the church to be built on. Another donated coconut trees for the lumber, another donated thatch for the roofing, and I donated a keg of nails we had left over after building our church in San Carlos. All the work was done by Filipinos. Of course, we held services while we were there and five others were saved and baptized at the same time as the grandmother. It was the first time I had ever preached barefooted (it would not be the last time) because my tennis shoes were still wet and everyone else was barefooted also. We spent that night sleeping on *benigs* (bamboo mats) rolled out on the floor. Our host, knowing that Americans usually slept on beds offered to let me roll out my *benig* on the dining table but I declined. I was afraid I would fall off the table and break my neck.

When we left to go back to San Carlos, they gave me a love offering, a live chicken and six eggs. To keep the eggs from being broken, I had them boil the eggs for us and we stopped and ate them about half way down the mountain. I carried that old chicken hen all the way back home to Cebu City.

The steady stream of visitors caused us to begin to search for property to build a church. We found a desirable piece of property just one block off the north/south National highway in the San Julio Subdivision. To own property in the Philippines, we would have to incorporate our church and record it as a Philippine corporation. I also had registered as a minister with the Philippine congressional library to officiate in marriages.

In June, 1973, we held a revival at the work in San Carlos. Our son, Mike, printed 1,000 revival flyers and we went on the radio with a 30-minute daily program advertising it. Rev. Ralph Baladhay, a Filipino preacher from Mandaue City, was our evangelist. We had about 150 first-time visitors for the week, and 59 were saved. I baptized 19 at the end of the revival. In our Children's church and extension classes there were 49 others saved, so the total for the week was 108 saved. On Saturday night of the revival, we had at least 300 in attendance. There were so many people in the building that it was impossible to get down the aisle. We took about 150 youngsters across the street to the City Plaza and taught them by the light of a kerosene lantern. We still had about 150 adults left in the church and it was wall to wall people.

On July 1, 1973, we formally organized from a mission to a church. We had baptized 93 since January 20th which was our first baptism service. In addition, we had four to join by letter and our family made three more, so we organized with exactly 100 members. In July we had averaged an attendance of 296.6 and ended July with 102 baptized.

The first of August, the Carter family took a break and went on vacation to Baguio City. The Filipinos kept up the good work while we were gone and set a new attendance record. They had 354 the first Sunday and 406 the next. This set a tradition for us. Every fall we took a vacation to relax from our hectic schedule.

A typical week included 4 hours of language school each week day for Harriett and me, several classes that we both taught in the Bible college, then leaving early Saturday morning on a bus to cross the Island of Cebu to Toledo, catch a ferry boat across 17 miles of open ocean to the Island of Negros. This normally would take five hours. We would stay in a hotel for the weekend, going out from there to visit, pass out tracts, and conduct extension classes in various barrios where we reached lots of children. We started church at 8:30am Sunday mornings in order for church to be over by 10:30am. That way people could go to the market, buy food, and then go home and cook it and eat near the noon hour. Evening service was held with light from kerosene lanterns and sometimes candles. There would be enough lights in the stores to guide us back to the hotel that ran a generator until about 10pm. At 4am on Monday morning we would walk through the dark streets and make our way to the ferry boat that would transport us back to the Island of Cebu. Then a bus ride across the island to Cebu City, where another week would start.

The ferry boat had a capacity of around 600. After we would get underway, I would pass out salvation tracts in the Cebuano language to everyone on board. Then I would take my seat. The ones who had questions would then come to me and I would be able to witness to them and show them how to be saved. This proved to be an effective way to win souls while traveling.

After the ferry boat would arrive in Toledo, if we needed to get on a bus, the real hassle began. The ferry could carry 600 passengers and there would normally be five or six 50 passenger buses to carry those going on to Cebu City. Harriett was not bold enough to get through, so I would get behind her and push her forward until we got to the door. Young boys made money by coming on the ferry, taking your suitcase, climb in the window of the bus and save you a seat. You still had to push your way on the bus to get to your seat. I have seen grown women wearing dresses climb in the windows of those buses.

Occasionally the ferry boat would not run and we would charter a *banca* (out-rigger canoe with a small gasoline engine) to make the crossing. This was not Harriett's favorite means of transportation, because we could see sharks in the water following us. The *banca* operator wanted 10 to 12 passengers to make as much money as possible. Some had canvas shades you could get under.

A new missionary family, Larry and Mary Waters and daughter moved to Cebu City to begin language study. In September, 1973, I invited him to come and speak at our new church. It was his first visit to the provincial part of the Philippines. I had him preach while Brother Vale interpreted for him. There were eight saved and four were baptized immediately after the services. On Saturday, we had gone all over San Carlos and its barrios teaching Good News classes and witnessing. We were in the Filipino homes and eating with the Filipinos and he was really excited. He told me, "Brother Carter, you are old enough to be my dad and you are working me to death. I don't see how you keep going." But the next day as we looked back on the souls that had been saved in the services, he said, "Now

I know how you keep going. I see what motivates you. I
that are getting saved." In his November prayer letter,
picture of him and the eight that had been saved, and anoi
of a blackboard out in front of our church where one of our Filipinos
had written, "Guest Speaker: Rev. Larry Waters (a young
missionary to the Philippines from America.). Come hear the Word
of God and be saved." That was the first time that I led the singing
in Cebuano. Before that, I had only led in the children choruses.
Larry and Mary Waters are still very dear friends. Harriett and I
became like grandparents for their two darling daughters.

Now that we were organized and registered as a Philippine
corporation, we finalized our land purchase and began serious
planning on building a church building. Dr. G. B. Vick of Detroit
Baptist Temple had given Missionary Bob Hughes $3,000 to use in
building a mission church in the Philippines and he donated it to the
Bible Baptist Church of San Carlos City. That was more than half
the total cost of our new building. We contracted with a lumber mill
to buy our lumber. It was managed by an American who sold us the
lumber at wholesale and then gave us a 25% discount. It made our
lumber cost about half what it would have cost in a local lumber
yard. The total cost for all the lumber was about $1,300.

Brother Hughes supplied me with a blueprint that he had used
to build a church somewhere else and we got a building permit from
the city. We were building a two-story building with the auditorium
upstairs, Sunday school rooms and a pastor's apartment downstairs.
It would have a concrete foundation, wooden frame, cement block
walls, wooden louver windows, and a tin roof.

The middle of December, 1973, work was started on our new
church building. Brother Hughes had a builder, Brother Ababon, in
his church that had built several buildings for him, so he became

.eman with his crew of builders. It is a learning experience to see Filipinos work and build with just hand tools. You cannot have electric tools if you don't have electricity. The lumber was saw mill rough and had to be planed smooth with hand planes. Sand, gravel, and cement was mixed by hand on site. But when they finished, they had done a beautiful job. The total time to build the church was four months.

In the meantime, we were using the rented store front building on the city plaza. This was still where we were meeting when my parents came to the Philippines to visit from the 21$^{st}$ of December until near the end of February, 1974. Brother Honeycutt's parents and my parents came together, and we all went to Manila to meet them and accompany them on down to Cebu City. My mother called it the trip of a lifetime. Once, when returning from Toledo to Cebu City, I had a flat on my pickup truck and the road had a couple of inches of mud on it. I stopped and was getting out my spare tire. I was dreading lying down in that mud to put the jack under the car when a couple of young Filipino men stopped and changed the tire for us. Then they would not take any pay for what they had done. My mother was very impressed with their selfless act of kindness. The last Sunday of 1973, our combined attendance, extension classes and church, was 676. We had a total of 1,106 souls saved and 166 baptisms in our first year at San Carlos City.

Our son Michael (Mike) Carter was such a blessing doing printing for us during his time in the Philippines. For his senior year of high school, he took a correspondence course for four hours every morning. Then he ran the print shop in the afternoon. He didn't have a plate burner but made a homemade one out of some plywood, a plate of glass, and some c-clamps. He used lights from a movie camera to expose the plate. He invented a way to make plates out of paper masters that cut the cost 90%. He wiped on a solution that is used for regrained plates and then burned an image on them just like metal plates. It worked like a charm and we could have 10 plates for the price of one.

During January and February, 1974, we continued building on the new church building while still holding services in the store front. As we built, we prayed for God to supply the materials. God was faithful. We paid every bill as it came due. Inflation caused the price to go over 10,000 pesos over the original estimate. Because there was no such thing as an "occupancy permit" in the Philippines at that time, we started meeting in the new building about the first of March. The roof was on and the flooring for the second-floor auditorium in, but there were no walls. We laid plywood on its side around the auditorium so the kids would not fall out and kill themselves and we had church services. We were in a building where the roof did not leak and our people were tickled to death with their new building.

Mike was now 18 years old and had graduated from high school. It was time for him to leave the Philippines and return to the States. Missionary Boyd Lyons and his family were going to leave on furlough on April 11, 1974, and arrangements were made for Mike to accompany the Lyons family so he would not have to go half way round the world by himself. One of the hardest things Harriett and I had ever done was watch our son walk across the apron of the airport to board that airplane. We had a bad case of the empty nest syndrome.

With Mike back in the States, we needed someone to run the printing operation. Brother Campos had surrendered his life at San Carlos and was attending Bible college in Cebu City. I trained brother Campos to run the printing operation. We printed 5,000

Cebuano song books, SS lessons, visual aids, gospel literature and tracts.

In June, Harriett and I went to San Carlos City for a week to lead our people in painting the church. We prepared a bed in the church office so we would not have to pay a hotel bill. The painters had put a bid in for 1,200 pesos for the labor to paint the church. That did not include the paint. A bunch of our young people came in and Harriett and I led them in the painting. On Tuesday of that week we had a Youth Fellowship meeting for the churches of Negros. During the service, a young man from our mission in Calatrava came and wanted to be baptized. As it turned out, he was both a painter and a sign painter. He came and painted for the rest of the week and painted us a beautiful sign across the back of the building toward the National Highway. We painted all the church, inside and out for a cost of 357 pesos for labor and 1,400 pesos for the paint.

It was during 1974 that the missions in Calatrava and Camaniangan were started with folks from those places who had been saved and baptized in San Carlos. Calatrava was following our example with extension classes and evangelistic services and was having good results. During June they reported 14 saved.

One Sunday morning soon after we had completed the San Carlos church building, a very old man came to the services. He walked all bent over and used a walking cane. He had grown up back when the Philippines was a colony of Spain, and the official language was Spanish. When I began talking to him, he replied in Spanish. I asked if he would talk to me in either Cebuano or English as I could not understand a lot of Spanish. Finally, I asked him his age and he replied in Spanish, *"Cien quatro"* which meant he was one hundred and four years old. I asked one of my preacher boys to talk to him also and ask his age in case I was mistaken. He came back a little later and said, "Pastor, he is one hundred and four years old." After the preaching service that morning when I started the invitation, the first thing I heard was the old man's walking cane on our wooden floor. He was responding to the invitation and was coming to get saved. Praise the Lord for allowing him to live long enough for someone to finally get the gospel message to him.

Another time, we had a new family come to visit our church. The church was still brand new, and we were so proud of it. I noticed them looking all around and I thought they were admiring our new building until they asked me, "Pastor, where are your gods?" They were looking for idols and I got to explain to them about our great invisible God that created the heavens and the earth.

Mission giving is as important on the mission field as it is in the States, so we began teaching faith promise giving to the Filipinos. Our first promise from our people was 200 pesos a month. It doesn't sound like much until you realize the average wage is seven pesos a day.

Brother Vale resigned as associate pastor to start a new work and I replaced him with Jun Canas, a graduate from the Bible school in Cebu City. He was very capable and a good preacher, which allowed me to preach at other places sometimes. We left on November 29, 1974 to preach the anniversary service for Missionary David Steffy at Bible Baptist Church of Tacloban on the island of Leyte on December 1st, returning to Cebu City on December 2nd. This was where General MacArthur came ashore when he fulfilled his promise to the Philippines, "I shall return." His footprints were embedded in concrete in front of the courthouse. Brother Steffy took me to White Beach where the actual invasion had taken place. There was still evidence of a terrific battle being fought there. There

45

were still rusted landing craft visible in the water where they had been disabled before they got all the way ashore.

Earlier, missionary Larry Waters had asked me to visit Legaspi to visit his family at Christmas time, to preach in the church there, and to preach on his television program. To get an airline ticket that near Christmas you must make your reservations 30 to 60 days in advance so we made reservations. We left on December 23$^{rd}$, flew to Manila, spent the night with the Woosleys, and then caught the airplane to Legaspi the next day. Then the problems began. When we got to Legaspi a typhoon had blown in and the plane was not able to land but returned to Manila. We had used our reservations and we were stuck at the airport in Manila. We could not go back home or go on to Legaspi. We rented a hotel room at the airport, went in every morning at 4am and put our names on the waiting list. We spent Christmas day at the airport. Finally, we got seats on to Legaspi, but our suitcases didn't make the flight. I preached in Legaspi in clothes I had worn several days. We did enjoy our time with the Waters. Instead of a stuffed turkey, Mary Waters stuffed about a 15-pound fish and baked it just like a turkey. It was so delicious.

Bob Hughes planned a city-wide crusade with Evangelist Jack Van Empe for Jan 19 – 25, 1975. This was going to be an all-out effort. Brother Hughes had recently finished the new church building for Cebu City which could seat three thousand. Our print shop printed 10,000 letters advertising the crusade. Missionaries from other places in the Philippines were coming and also Brother Jack Bridges, former mission director and now a pastor in Houston, came for the crusade. Al Young, business man out of Detroit Baptist Temple, came also. Brother Hughes delegated me the job of showing Al Young and Jack Van Empe the sights of Cebu City. My pickup was getting beat up from the rough roads I was driving on.

The radiator leaked. I had to carry water and add some to the radiator ever so often. To their credit Jack Van Empe and Al Young never said a thing.

While we were in the market at Cebu City, an army jeep came through with a loud speaker making announcements in the Cebuano language. I really was not paying attention to what they were saying until Jack Van Empe asked me what they were saying. When I began to pay attention, I learned that a typhoon was to hit that evening. This was about the third night of the crusade. Brother Van Empe asked me how it was going to affect the Crusade. I replied that it would be a big problem. Brother Van Empe then joked, referring to businessman Al Young, "Now I can say I have been in a typhoon with a tycoon."

That evening, services started as usual with Brother Van Empe playing his electric accordion and His wife singing specials. There were 2,500 in attendance even with the typhoon warning. Then the typhoon hit and the lights all went out along with all sound equipment. Deacons were prepared and quickly put up candles and lanterns around the auditorium. But we had a problem, how were thousands of people going to hear Brother Van Empe's soft voice without a sound system. A decision was made. Brother Baladhay, Filipino pastor from Mandaue preached. He had a loud enough voice that he could be heard even though a typoon was raging outside. When the invitation was given over 200 people got saved.

After the service my job was to take some of the visitors to where they were staying. I drove Brother Bridges and Brother Van Empe to the Hughes house and then brought Brother and Sister Steffy home with me where they were staying in our guest bedroom. I had to drive carefully because of the heavy rain and 100 mile-an-hour wind. Trees were blown down in the roads and the roads were littered with debris.

We finally made it home about midnight. The wind was blowing at hurricane strength. When we tried to light a kerosene lamp, there was too much draft. We discovered a louvered window had been blown open in my office. After closing that, we were able to light the lamp, and Harriett made sandwiches for our guests, David and Uldine Steffy. While we were eating, it suddenly became very quiet. The wind had quit blowing! It had gone from 100 miles an hour to zero, we were in the eye of the storm! It was an eerie feeling, so quiet. Brother Steffy and I walked outside and the sky seemed gray instead of black. After the eye went over the wind hit again.

The next morning, we assessed the damage. Our house was intact, but we had a lot of tree damage. We had a big mango tree in our yard and the top was broken off and down. Two other fruit trees were damaged also. Across our side fence, an entire banana orchard was flat on the ground.

When Brother Hughes had visitors from the States, he used that opportunity to have them preach in the schools, colleges, and universities. Brother Van Empe preached in these various schools and there were 850 saved. At the church services there were 1,209 saved, for a total of 2,059 saved for the week.

Our San Carlos associate pastor, Jun Canas took typhoid fever and had to have time off, eventually resigning. Brother Yerro took the pastor position in March 1975.

With a Filipino pastor in San Carlos, I began concentrating my efforts on Calatrava. The one who had been in charge of the work there had moved from that town. Harriett and I rented a room every weekend from the grandfather of a girl named Phoebe Sennarillos, who had been one of the first from Calatrava to come to San Carlos to be saved. Her story was extremely sad. A few years earlier her father had come home drunk and killed her mother with a machete right in front of all the children. The kids had been split up and sent to live with relatives. Phoebe had come to live with her grandparents. Phoebe thought no one loved her. When she found out that Jesus loved her it transformed her life. In her mind, she adopted Harriett and I as her adopted parents. I used Jun Villaflor as an accordion teacher for Phoebe. She learned to play, but her brother, Adam Sennarillos, was the one who became a master at playing an accordion. He later went to, and graduated from, the Bible college in Cebu. While he was there I paid for him to take piano lessons. I thought he would be a natural as a music director.

Brother Jaunito Nueva, a Bible college graduate, had come to Calatrava in March to be the associate pastor. In the Spring of 1975, we rented an old gasoline station as a place to hold services in Calatrava. It would only hold about 50 or 60 but the walls were slotted where you could see inside from the outside. We planned on having an evangelistic meeting right away to get everyone's attention. It just so happened that Rev. Roy Wallace and his wife, Helen, from Center, Texas were visiting us at that time. Brother Wallace helped us wire the building so we could use our generator and have lights. Then he preached the first service of the evangelistic meeting. It was raining that night, the building was packed out, and hordes of people were standing outside in the rain to hear him speak. This had a profound effect on Brother Wallace. With tears in his eyes, Brother Wallace said, "I have trouble back in Center getting people to come to church when it is raining where they have a dry place to sit. And here people are standing in the rain to hear me preach." Final count, 27 saved.

49

Another girl who was from Calatrava was Melene Loguelogue. She had surrendered her life and also attended the Bible college in Cebu. Harriett and I would take these two girls and go to the different areas in Calatrava and hold extension classes every Saturday. Then on Sundays we would hold church services. We usually had around 400 to 500 in the extensions classes and then a little over 100 in the church services for a weekly attendance of 600 to 650 in Calatrava.

Harriett and I started praying about moving from Cebu City to San Carlos. It would save 10 hours of traveling each week. The electric company in San Carlos had started supplying electricity from 12 noon until about 10pm. We just needed to find a house to rent.

In July, Pastor Yerro resigned as pastor of Bible Baptist Church in San Carlos to take a church that had come open on the island of Leyte. Now it became urgent that we relocate to San Carlos. This was a lot harder than just renting a U-Haul trailer. We moved in about a week and a half after I made up my mind to move. The first thing we had to do was crate all our things for shipment in a boat. That meant I had to take down all that pipe the plumber put on the back of my house for the hot water heater. I made about 12 wooden crates and then we wrapped all the furniture in cardboard. We had over 100 pieces of freight. Everything was trucked to the dock and then loaded onto an inter-island steamer. We had our pickup truck loaded down also. We drove to Toledo, and put the truck on the ferry boat. I had to meet the inter-island steamer that had our things on it. When we got to San Carlos, the dock was congested with ships and freight and they couldn't unload my pickup. The ferry tied up to a ship that was tied up to the dock. The passengers on the ferry had to cross off the ferry, go across the deck of the other ship, and then down a gangplank to the dock. The pickup made five round trips between Toledo and San Carlos before it was finally unloaded.

When the ship with our belongings arrived, I hired a truck and workers to haul our things from the docks to the church in San Carlos. We were going to live in the pastor apartment until we found a house to rent. We were supposed to have a house to move into about the middle of September. Mormon missionaries had rented a house about a block from our church about a year before. We joked and said we were going to pray them out of that house so we could have it to live in. Lo and behold, they moved out on the 15th and the owner rented the house to us. That was one more move, but it was only a block away.

After moving into our house, I had it screened in as protection from mosquitoes. A lot of things were different living in San Carlos. The best the electricity ever did was stay on half the time. It was supposed to come on at noon but sometimes it did not come on until dark and sometimes not at all. The deep freeze did not work as everything thawed out while the electricity was off. The refrigerator did pretty well. We had a Coleman ice chest set up in the kitchen with ice in it all the time. Every night, we took out everything we were going to need for breakfast and lunch and put it in the ice box. That way the refrigerator was never opened while the electricity was off. Generally, if the electricity came on at noon we could open the refrigerator and the ice cubes would still be frozen.

There was not a good meat market. We bought our meat at an open-air market. A quarter of beef, or possibly water buffalo, would be hung out in the open. I would get them to cut off a chunk and then take it home and cut it up into some semblance of slices. I had a meat grinder that I tried to make hamburger meat on but the meat was just too tough. It would not grind it.

Our Dodge pickup had an 8' bed with a shell camper. Inside we had built bench seats down both sides and across the front. Then we put a bench down the center. It would haul a lot of weight and a lot of people. I put on heavier springs and larger tires to carry all the weight. One time I came in with a load and Harriett counted the people that got out of and off of that pickup. The total was 55! Of course, most were children, but 8 of us were stacked in the cab. That still meant that 47 were from inside the camper or standing on the back bumper.

In August, 1975, we got some bad news from Cebu City. Missionary Bob Hughes was in the hospital with colon cancer. He had been having pain in his stomach a long time and his doctor had misdiagnosed his problem as amoeba. I went to visit him in the hospital in Cebu City, and he ended up comforting me rather than me comforting him. The Hughes family returned to the States to try to find a cure for the cancer. One blessing was that he was able to win some of his brothers to the Lord that he had been praying for several years. Missionary Ralph LaRosa came to fill in at Cebu City.

The first of September, I preached revival services at Balintawak for Brother Vale who had a new mission there. On Friday evening, as Harriett and I were going there, the automatic transmission on our pickup quit. We left the truck on the side of the road and caught a jeepney the rest of the way. After the service, I went back to the truck with some automatic transmission fluid. It would go for a little way and then quit. We finally got home at 11:15pm. On Saturday morning I overslept and forgot to go to the radio station to make our weekly radio broadcast. Shame on me. I badly needed the vacation I took from October 1st until the 21st in Baguio City.

In November, a small feeder airline started serving San Carlos. A five-hour trip to Cebu now was a 15-minute flight. We also had a telephone installed in our house. The automatic transmission was still a problem. There was not an auto garage on Negros that knew how to work on them. They removed it from the pickup and shipped it Cebu City to have it repaired. There were no parts in Cebu City, but they were going to check if parts were available from Manila. To get around, I bought a small 100 cc Kawasaki motorcycle. I rode it and Harriett would get on behind me side saddle, Filipino style. The roads were so bad we could only go about 12 miles per hour. It had a luggage rack, and when we bought groceries, we would tie them on the luggage rack. It was our main means of transportation and for going on visitation.

I invited the Larry Waters family to visit us for Christmas at San Carlos. For the Waters two daughters, DeAnna and Dawn, I made a Christmas tree out of a big dry weed that I found. I wrapped all the weed in green crepe paper and decorated it like a Christmas tree. I put cotton around the base to make it look like snow. Brother Waters was our special speaker at our Christmas Eve service. There were nearly 400 in the building and 17 were saved.

In January 1976, I bought a small generator from Delbert Hooge, the missionary at Cavite. It was big enough to run the well pump, run the house electricity, and operate either the washing machine or the clothes dryer. It was not powerful enough to run washer and dryer at the same time. Overload. I installed a two-way throw entrance switch that let me select the city electricity if it was on, or the generator. If I was running the generator, I did not know when the city electricity came on. I installed a 10-watt red light hooked to the city electric and solved that problem. If the red light came on, I switched to the city electric.

53

At the beginning of February, I met a man with a house to sell in Calatrava. He had built it for his home, but he had not yet put in the dividing walls upstairs and it would make a perfect auditorium. On the 12$^{th}$ of February I rode the motorcycle to Calatrava and bought the place for an equivalent of $3,500. My daughter and her husband, Kathy and Larry Bice had given $1,000 to apply to the purchase and churches had responded to my pleas with the rest of the money. The downstairs would be SS rooms and the pastor apartment. One of my Sunday School teachers, Phoebe Sennarillos, had fallen in love with Pastor Nueva and they were married about the end of March.

I had been announcing to our Filipino people, that we had to go home to the States in April to report to our supporting churches. One of my older men, Phoebe's grandfather, thought we did not want to go back to the States and he started a petition getting people to sign that they did not want us to have to return to the States. When I found out about it, I told him that we were looking forward to going back so that we could see our parents and our kids and grandkids. He was satisfied when I told him that and dropped the petition idea.

The transmission was working again on my Dodge pickup. But then the electronic ignition burned up. Dad sent new parts from the States but after the mechanic installed them, it still would not run. The mechanic called in a television repair man and he made a homemade resistor and the engine fired up. I could use my pickup again. It had been repaired Filipino style.

God had put a desire in my heart to build a church in Bacolod, a city on the west coast of Negros island, on our next term. I made a survey trip with Brother Ralph LaRosa to Bacolod City. On the way home, we stopped in a small city and had lunch. When we came back to the truck, it would not start. I raised the hood and the resistor had burned up. It was just ashes. While I was looking at it several Filipinos were watching. They began to tell me where to find a mechanic. They were dumbfounded when I told them I did not need a mechanic, I needed a television repair man. They kept saying that I needed a mechanic, not a television repair man. I finally had to close the hood and go into a store where they didn't know I was having car problems, and ask for the address of a television repairman. When I finally got a television repairman, I had to convince him that he could repair my pickup truck. He made me a new resistor and I went on my way. We had much more trouble on that trip when the battery box broke, shorting out the battery, because of the rough roads. Prayer got us home.

In one of our first services in Calatrava, Phoebe's grandfather had come forward and made a profession of faith. On one of my weekends in Calatrava, Phoebe told me that her grandfather had told her he was not saved. He was sick in bed when I went to talk to him. He told me that when he came forward he was not sincere, that he was holding something back. I told him we could pray right then for God to save him. But he resisted saying that he wanted to think about it and be absolutely sure. I felt as if I were personally wrestling with the devil as I witnessed and tried to get grandfather to accept Christ. I kept praying for him but had almost given up when he got out of his sickbed, kneeled down by his bed, and asked God to save his soul. Praise the Lord for the victory.

## Chapter 6 – **First Furlough**

In April 1976, a large group of members from the San Carlos church went to the dirt airport that the feeder airline used, to tell us goodbye. We flew from San Carlos to Cebu City, then took a jet to Manila. From Manila we flew on a charter flight to Los Angeles. We had adapted to the tropics after years in the Philippines. I was wearing a wool suit I had a tailor make for me in the Philippines. I had walked to the airplane with the suit coat over my arm and only put it on after I got on the airconditioned airplane. We arrived in L.A. about 2am local time. The temperature outside was 60 degrees and long before we got to the door I was already feeling the cold. Our charter flight did not have a gate and the plane unloaded at a shed right out in the open on the back side of the airport. There were buses there to take us to the main terminal. We could load on the buses only after we got our baggage. We were both freezing. It was going to take a while to unload all that luggage so Harriett and I prayed that our luggage would be on the first load. God answered our prayer and we got aboard the first bus where the driver had the heater running.

Back at the terminal, we were having a hard time adjusting to the American culture. It had been so long since we had seen Americans, it seemed like I should know everyone I met. We were still bowing to people, speaking English with a Philippine accent and were acting like Filipinos. We rented a locker for our luggage and when the young lady gave me the key, I bowed and said, "Thank you Ma'am (which pronounces exactly like Mom in English)." I don't know what the young lady thought about an older man calling her mom so I just bowed again and turned around and left.

After a six-hour layover, we caught a flight to El Paso, Texas. We were surprised to see a large group of people from the Bel-Aire

Baptist Church holding a banner, "Welcome Home Missionaries." We had been 48 hours in route and had not been to bed. Then Pastor Dean Lang told me that we had arrived during their mission conference. Then he said, "You are preaching tonight."

After eating lunch at my parents' house, we went to bed for a few hours' sleep before the mission conference. That evening, in my introductory remarks, I related calling the young lady "mom" and told them I was still thinking in Filipino and to excuse my way of speaking. Even when we were speaking in English, there were some Philippine words we always used. For thank you we always said *daghan salamat*. Brother was always *brad*. A lady that we didn't personally know was *inday*. I got through the sermon, but I highly recommend several weeks in the States before an attempt is made to preach in order for the missionary to adjust back to the American culture and language.

After resting up a few days while visiting my folks in El Paso, we continued to Dallas, Texas. We had put up a map of the United States and put pins at ever supporting church. Dallas was about the center of all our churches so it made sense to settle there. One of the members of Bruton Road Baptist Church managed an apartment complex across the street from it and she rented us an unfurnished apartment.

We had been well advised on culture shock when going to a foreign mission field. We had been also well advised on what to take to the field with us. Nothing was said of reverse culture shock when returning to the States. And nothing was said of what missionaries returning to the States for furlough would need. Both of these were a shock to us. We were in Dallas and all we owned was in our suitcases. We scrounged up some used furniture and the apartment manager loaned us a dinette set. Brother David Hardy led the members of Eastland Baptist Church to gather up things that we would need. Things like coffee pot, frying pans, baking pans, etc. They sent them to Dallas with Brother Lee Ingram. Harriett and I sat down in the middle of the living room and began to unpack the things Eastland had sent. Every time we would pull something out of the box, Harriett would exclaim, "Oh, that's just what we need." Later when I was telling Brother Hardy about it, he said, "How could we miss? You needed everything."

We had been given an old Toyota automobile to use while in the States but it turned out to be unreliable. Eastland Baptist Church was still meeting in a store front because of the tornado that destroyed their church. We were going to their mission conference and the Toyota broke down in Atoka, Oklahoma. We missed the first part of their conference and decided we needed to buy a better car. We bought a car that Hertz car rental had retired and used that throughout our furlough.

While still in the Philippines, I had written my supporting churches and told of my upcoming furlough and asked to come to their mission conference if possible. I even had the audacity to ask if they wanted me to be their main speaker. I came back to the States with 30 mission conferences scheduled with more than half of them having me as the main speaker. It made my furlough really hard work with lots of driving. Harriett and I split up the driving. She did half of the driving while I drove the other half. In the mid-seventies, showing slides was the preferred method of telling about the field. I explained about the slide then showing instead of having a recording. That way you could vary the slides every time they were shown, emphasizing what needed to be emphasized each time.

At the Spring Fellowship meeting in May, 1976, in Springfield, Missouri in one of the mission committee meetings, Brother Carl

Boonstra, Fellowship Mission Director, read a letter from Missionary Larry Waters recommending that the Carters be reconsidered as Fellowship missionaries. He then presented the proposition to the mission committee members and they approved Brother Boonstra asking me to reapply for status as a Fellowship missionary. When I told Harriett of us being asked to reapply, she said, "We were too old to be missionaries five years ago, did we get younger?" We reapplied as there are many advantages of being a Fellowship missionary; one of which is that they are so well vetted that everyone knew what they stood for. Another is a dedicated mission office that acts as your clearing house and with good people who have your back.

Eddie Gerodias, a graduate of Cebu City Bible College, was now pastor of Bible Baptist Church of San Carlos during our furlough. He came there as a young man and stuck it out through thick and thin. He made that his life work. God used him to make Bible Baptist the church it is today. We had kept our rental home in the Philippines and left Jing-Jing Usaraga, my secretary, in charge of the house and also paying our bills while we were gone. She did a wonderful job. Our pickup truck was left up on blocks in the carport.

Back in the Philippines, the devil was still fighting our churches. Some of the hacienda owners were threatening their laborers who attended the Baptist church in Calatrava with being fired and evicted from their homes if they continued to attend. Some quit going to church, but one man, Brother Ugdiman kept going to church. He was in turn fired and evicted just as he had been threatened.

Brother Ugdiman found a new job and new housing in a mountain village named Magazine. He started soul winning in that town and gathered quite a group. The church at Calatrava sponsored him to start a mission in that town. One man donated an acre of ground for a church building and God blessed their efforts. They began regular church services. In a one-month period, Brother Ugdiman reported 10 saved and nine waiting for baptism.

Meanwhile back in the States, I was crisscrossing the country preaching in mission conferences and trying to raise support in new churches. During this furlough I would preach in 108 churches and participate in 30 mission conferences, drive 50,000 miles plus some airline trips, and a couple of trips where I flew a rented airplane to preach to churches in New Mexico.

In August, 1976, I was staying with my daughter, Gloria, and son-in-law and preaching at churches in Ohio. Pastor Harold Henniger of Canton Baptist Temple had an appointment in Kentucky and asked me to be the speaker at their Wednesday evening service. Of course, I jumped at the chance to preach in one of the largest churches in America. There would be about 2,000 in attendance on a Wednesday service. Then I got the sad news that Bob Hughes had died and they were having his funeral. I wanted to go to the funeral but it would have been almost impossible to make it on time. I prayed about it and decided that I should keep my appointment at Canton Baptist Temple. I believe that is what Brother Hughes would have wanted me to do.

At the September, 1976 meeting of the Baptist Bible Fellowship in Indianapolis, Indiana, the Carters were approved as Fellowship missionaries. Doctor Cavin and High Street Baptist Church had been our sponsor on our first term. The supporting churches had all sent their support directly to High Street. Now all that had to be redirected to the Mission office. This took a lot of work off of Doctor Cavin's secretary who deposited all the checks and sent me receipts of the checks so that I could write them and thank them for the support and prayers.

My oldest daughter, Gloria, and her husband, Rev. Lowell Haggerty lived in Canton, Ohio. Lowell and his father, Rev. Jack Haggerty, promoted our ministry among the churches of Ohio. Gloria and Lowell invited me to stay in their home and preach in Ohio. Our two best supporting states were Texas and Ohio. It was during this furlough that Rev. Lowell Haggerty was called as pastor of Lake Milton Baptist Temple. I was in Ohio and was able to drive the truck that hauled their furnishings from Canton to Lake Milton.

Although Texas and Ohio were our best supporting States, we had supporting churches from Washington state to California on the west coast and from Florida to Vermont on the east coast. It took lots of traveling to report to all of our churches. We almost worked ourselves to death on that first furlough, and I never again sent out a letter to set up an itinerary before we came back to the States. From that time, I planned my itinerary so that I could visit all the churches in a particular area while I was there. My planning did not always work, as some pastors wanted me in their mission conferences and I made concessions so that I could accommodate them.

During this furlough, I was presenting the vision of a new work in Bacolod City, the city I had surveyed while still in the Philippines. We were also trying to buy the things we would need that were not available in the Philippines. We were not able to buy shoes big enough to fit in the Philippines. Neither could we buy clothing our sizes.

To write prayer letters I was able to purchase a Flex-o-writer and a second reader. This was before computers were available for personal use. A Flex-o-writer was a teletype kind of automatic typewriter that used a paper strip with holes punched in it to write letters. One reader had the address code and the other reader had the letter code. When you typed the prayer letter you inserted switch codes to switch between readers. You could also put in a stop code if you intended to write something personal to a particular church. When it was all set up, it typed about 100 words per minute and made a lot of noise. Printing a monthly prayer letter took on the average about eight hours.

Rev. David Hardy and Eastland Baptist Church gave us another printing press for the printing ministry. It was a Multilith 1250 that had survived the tornado. It would eventually print out a wealth of material for the Philippine churches. We rented a storage space in Dallas to store these things until we would take them to the west coast.

Dallas proved to be a good location for family. Harriett's mother, two sisters lived in Dallas, and a brother lived nearby. We had three grandchildren born while we were in Bible College. We had three grandchildren born on our first term and we were able to meet them and get to know them. Donna Kay was born to our daughter Sandra, and was about three when we first saw her. When we arrived at their home in Tennessee, everyone ran out to the car to hug us. I noticed Donna Kay hanging back. We were complete strangers to her. I squatted down and held out my arms and said, "Donna, I am Pawpaw." Then she ran to me and gave me a big hug. Michelle was born to our daughter Kathy and was almost two when we first met her. Jennifer Renee was born to our son, Mike and was only a few months old. While we were home on furlough Kathy gave birth to twins, Melanie and Melody. Mike's son, Jacob Michael, would be born while we were on our next term back in the Philippines.

While on our furlough, we had a family reunion in Tennessee at Sandra's house and celebrated our 30th wedding anniversary. We were also able to attend my parents 50<sup>th</sup> wedding anniversary in El Paso, Texas. In June, all our children and grandchildren gathered at Alto, Texas to see us one last time before we went home to the Philippines. It was hard to leave them, but God had given us a job to do in the Philippines.

The furlough seemed to fly by, and with all the preaching engagements and traveling, we were exhausted. My daughter, Kathy, and her husband bought the car we had used on furlough. We crated up the things that we had gathered to use in the Philippines and rented a U-Haul truck and started for California. The truck was not airconditioned and we sweltered going across the desert in Arizona. The wind was blowing so hot as we were crossing western Arizona, that it was hotter with the windows open than it was when they were closed. We had a gallon thermos of water and we drank the whole gallon as we crossed the desert.

Roy Hendrickson of Fellowship Missionary and Crating Service had arranged with some stores to sell supplies to missionaries at a reduced price. We bought the supplies we needed including a dish washer, cookstove and a new refrigerator. We had also gathered several accordions and at least one guitar to use in the churches. Brother Hendrickson and I made several 4' X 4' X 8' crates to pack the printing press and everything else in. We would reuse the lumber in these crates to make things we needed when we got to the Philippines.

This time, instead of going by ship, we went by air. It took so much less time and we were home-sick to be back home in the Philippines. The crates would come by ship and would be several months behind us getting to the Philippines.

## Chapter 7 – **Philippines Second Term**

When our airplane landed at the dirt strip in San Carlos City, we found a large group of our church members there to welcome us home. Some had taken off work to be there. Not knowing how hard we had worked on furlough, they asked, "How did you enjoy your vacation?" They did not know that I had to come home to get rested up.

Jing-Jing had done an excellent job of handling our finances and everything was paid up and there was money in the bank. I changed the oil in the pickup's motor, took out the sparkplugs, and rotated the engine before I reinstalled the sparkplugs and cranked it up. I spent the next couple of weeks preaching at San Carlos and Calatrava. Phoebe's grandmother was saved when I preached at Calatrava. Her grandfather had died the day we left on furlough.

Both churches were now under National pastors making me free to pioneer a work in Bacolod. We went there and began searching for a house suitable both to live in and to have services there also. We checked with real estate companies looking for rental houses. Brother Consino had a jeepney, and we drove around town looking for a suitable house for rent. As we drove down Tacoling Street, I noticed a large house that just looked vacant. I knocked but there was no one home, so I went to a neighboring house to inquire. The house had belonged to a fairly wealthy man who had gone bankrupt and the house had been repossessed. I went to the bank that now owned it and was able to rent it from them.

We turned our rent house in San Carlos City back over to its owner, who wanted to live in it himself. We held a final service in San Carlos where all the people came and told us "goodbye." Many were crying, even though I told them I was still their missionary, but Pastor Eddie Gerodias was going to be their pastor from then on.

They asked Harriett and me to stand at the front of the church, and they all lined up and came by hugging us and telling us their last "goodbyes." There were some young men that you could not have made cry by torturing them, that were crying.

Our crates arrived in Manila and we had them sent directly to Bacolod. We contracted a truck to move our belongings from San Carlos to Bacolod. As the electric service in the Philippines is 220 volts, we had to install a transformer to transform the service outlets to 110 volts where we would plug in our things from America. All the overhead lighting remained at 220 volts. We found a piano we could buy, and moved it into the living room. Now we had a place to live and also a place to start a church.

One thing we did not know about the house, the Filipinos thought the house was haunted. They said old tires would roll around in the yard at night with no one rolling them. As we were moving our belongings from the crates to the three bedrooms, we noticed some irregularities. When we would take things in to the front bedroom, we would leave the door open as we went to get another load, and when we would return, the door would be closed. We would open the door and stand there and watch it and it would stay open, but when we would leave to get something else to bring in, it would be closed again. I had made a curio display case out of the plywood of our crates, and Harriett was putting her little curios on display. One was a little ceramic dog. She would place the little dog facing the room, but the next time she would go in the room the dog would be turned around facing the wall. This happened multiple times. It would make the hair stand up on your neck but we knew that *"Greater is He that is in you, than he that is in the world."* 1 John 4:4. A few weeks in a house that was also used as a church and the demons left. When we started in Bacolod, the church met in our house. Before it was over, we lived in the church. We were awakened many times from our siesta with specials being practiced.

Our house had three bedrooms and we chose to make the middle bedroom a private living room. We called it the Music Room. We had brought some carpet from America that we installed. We put in Harriett's desk, our stereos, a couch and chair. The room was quiet enough that I recorded my radio tapes there. The recorders, mixer, and microphone were all set up in there. The radio ministry had proved profitable in San Carlos, so we instituted a radio ministry in Bacolod City also.

On August 28, 1977, we had our first service with an attendance of 50. The first Sunday in September, 47 attended in the middle of a big rain storm. In the two weeks, we had 31 accept Christ as their Savior. The next four weeks the attendance grew every week, 71, 74, 97, and 105. Thirty-eight saved and 13 baptized in one month. In the first four weeks of services, our Filipinos had given 500 pesos in offerings and I had not had much time to preach on giving. We had to buy a lot of chairs to seat all the folks that were coming. There was a large garage with an open front at the end of the driveway and this was used as a Sunday School room. Another building housed the printing press and the dark room for making printing plates.

We installed our hot water heater and the automatic dishwasher that we had brought in our crates. My secretary, Jing-Jing, was amazed that a machine could actually wash dishes. Her comment, "Americans are not only loving, they are geniuses."

Brother LaRosa was leaving for the States on furlough and I bought his 1971 Toyota sedan and his 100 cc Honda motorcycle. The Toyota was a tough little car, and I turned the motorcycle over to the youth pastor, Nonoy Jamilo.

Missionary Larry Waters was on furlough in the States. He asked me to go to Naga City and preach to the church there. He had left the work in the capable hands of a Filipino preacher. The attendance when I was there was 350 and there were 20 saved that day and seven baptized. Back in Bacolod, I had asked Pastor Eddie Gerodias from San Carlos to be our speaker. There were 14 saved.

Shortly after starting using our Dodge pickup, the automatic transmission quit working again. Probably not being used for a year had something to do with it. An auto parts store in Bacolod had Toyota engines and transmission combinations that had been taken out of vehicles in Japan. I bought one and had the Dodge engine and transmission replaced with the Toyota engine and transmission. The original pickup had no clutch so they made one out of the brake pedal. They just sawed it into with a hacksaw and attached it to a new clutch arm. This also cured the problem of having to have a TV repairman make resistors. Now instead of getting around 10 miles per gallon, I was getting better than 20 miles per gallon. I had to get used to shifting the gears because the transmission had come out of a Japanese car with right hand steering. Now in a vehicle that steered from the left seat the shifting pattern was reversed. This truck was used similar to a bus ministry in the States. I also used it to transport cases of Bibles and to go to Fellowship meetings when I wanted to take multiple workers along. Every time it made a trip there was always many who wanted to go along.

A new work must be grounded in Bible doctrine. Every time a new work was started, I preached a series of doctrinal messages. The first message was always, "There is a God." This God had given us His Word, the Bible. The Bible tells of Jesus, God's Son who was the Savior. The Holy Spirit completed the Trinity. There is an enemy, the devil. There is a heaven and there is a hell. I would preach a separate sermon on the ten major points of theology. I think too many pastors in the States presume their people already know all of this. Get real, they don't.

In December, 1977, the devil was mad and started trouble. The problem came from my associate pastor's wife. They had learned we were coming to Bacolod to start a work and after graduating from Bible College, they had been holding a Bible study in their home waiting for us to come. She was a strong woman and she had been running the Bible study. Now I had started the new church and I was running things and she did not like it. She wanted to run the church. She started a whisper campaign trying to undermine the missionaries. First, I went to her husband and told him to control his wife. He said he would talk to her, but he was afraid to confront her, and one evening she started on me. When I related that I had already spoken to her husband about her activities, she was angry. She quit the church and in a few weeks, she had made the rest of her family to quit also. It was sad because I had been training her son to run the printing press, and her daughter was a gifted pianist.

Missionary Boyd Lyons and his wife Donna had promised they would come to Bacolod after we had the church going to teach our new teachers and to preach a revival. They came in February, 1978, and stayed in our guest room. One of our members was a good artist. He made a large poster with a drawing of a male lion and a lioness. He then labeled it "The Lyons Den." We put this poster on the door of their bedroom. Boyd and Donna were with us for a week and God blessed. Donna performed her chalk talk and Brother Lyons preached powerful messages. On the last night the attendance was 150! The living room was packed solid, people were sitting on benches on the front porch looking through the door, and there were folks at every window. For that month there were 82 saved and 13 baptized.

In Bacolod, it was too far to go to the ocean to baptize so we baptized in the rivers. Usually there would be Carabao (water buffalo) lying in the river cooling off and usually there were women folks there washing their clothes in the river. The baptisms were also a form of witnessing. I usually read about baptisms from the Bible and then spoke about the meaning of baptism. That way, the onlookers got a short lesson.

We built a thatch shelter in the back yard for young people's Sunday School. When it was not raining the juniors were taught under a shade tree, and the primaries were taught in the garage building. The house was bursting at the seams with an attendance nearing 200 on Sunday mornings. We taught in different barrios on Saturdays in extension classes but did not include that count in our total attendance.

At last we found property to purchase to build a church building on. It was across the road from our house and about half a block away. It had 129 feet of frontage and 96 feet deep. In April, 1978, we purchased it paying 50% down with the balance coming due in September. We did not need property for a large parking lot as there were few automobiles owned by our congregation.

How were we going to pay for the size building we needed to house the people we were reaching? I made a list of all of our supporting churches and went into my prayer closet. I prayed over each church and asked God what He wanted them to give. When God would give an answer, I wrote it down and went to the next church repeating the process. Then I wrote the name of each church, the name of the pastor, and the amount God wanted them to give on a 5 X 7 card. I then asked for volunteers in our church who would be faithful to pray every day for that church to give that amount. Each volunteer had a special church that only they prayed for. The one exception was Berean Baptist Church in Albuquerque, New Mexico. God wanted them to give $10,000. I made several cards for Berean and Harriett and I took one and gave one to each staff member of the church.

When the first offering came in, it was for $1,000 and it was the exact amount God had laid on my heart for that church. When we had our next service, I asked who had been given that church to pray for. One of our teenage girls, Jean Barley, raised her hand. I asked her in a serious manner, "Have you been faithful in praying for this church every day?" She answered, "Yes, Pastor." I then asked, "Have you prayed they would give $1,000?" Again, she answered, "Yes, Pastor." Then I told her, "Your prayers have been answered. You have prayed down $1,000 to help build our church." That would have been about a year's wages for most of our people. Almost every church sent in the amount we prayed for. Even the $10,000 came in from Berean Baptist Church. After the new building was finished, one of my men said, "Pastor Carter, this is the church that prayer built."

In May, 1978, the number of churches and missions on the island of Negros had grown to fifteen. We held the first ever Bible Baptist Youth Camp on our island and invited young people from all fifteen churches. There were 105 campers, and 19 surrendered their lives for full time service. Thirteen of those 19 were out of our church in Bacolod.

In September, 1978, the Bible Baptist Church of Bacolod City was organized. We were still meeting in our house. The attendance on organization day was 278 and 108 baptized members signed our charter. Our property was fully paid for and there was an architect drawing the plans for our new building. Groundbreaking ceremony was held in November.

Another thing we started on our second term was a Pastors and Workers Fellowship meeting every month for the Island of Negros. One thing missionaries and pastors need is to hear good sound preaching. We prepare and preach sermons constantly, but there is a need to be preached to. Canton Baptist Temple sent us a cassette each week with Pastor Harold Henniger preaching. Harriett and I would go to our private place and listen to Pastor Henniger preach each week. With a backlog of those cassettes, I bought cassette players for all our preachers. At the fellowship meetings I would loan out four sermons to each pastor, and at the next fellowship meeting they would return the cassettes and check out four more. Different churches hosted the fellowship meetings each month, with the preachers who were to preach being notified beforehand. This fellowship meeting was an encouragement to each one that attended.

At year's end of 1978, the work in Bacolod was organized and we had started two new missions out of the new church. Total saved during 1978 in these three works were 681 with 146 baptized. The combined attendance of all our works on Negros rose to 1,380 in the last quarter of the year.

One day I received a call from the pastor at San Carlos. He told me that Brother Ugdiman was very, very sick with malaria fever. This was the man who had been fired from his job and evicted from his home for attending the Baptist church at Calatrava, then went to another place and started a new work. One of Brother Ugdiman's members had brought news of his condition to Pastor Eddie Gerodias. We made plans for Pastor Eddie to contact the pastor at Calatrava, his sending church, and then they would ride a bus to where the road went up into the mountains. I would meet the two of them there with my car, and we would go into the mountains and take Brother Ugdiman to the hospital.

The road into the mountains was very primitive. At one place, all the planking was off a bridge across a narrow but deep gorge. The main beams were still there stretching across the gorge. Fortunately, they matched enough that with Brother Eddie guiding me, I drove across the gorge on those two beams. When we arrived at Brother Ugdiman's home, it was about ½ kilometer from the road. His wife related to me that her husband had told her he was dying. When I went to him he said, "Pastor Carter, about this time tomorrow I am going to be with the Lord." I answered, "No, you are not. We are all going to kneel here by your *benig* and pray for your recovery and then take you to the hospital." After our prayer, we carried him the ½ kilometer back to the car, then drove back down that perilous road to a hospital where he was admitted.

After about one week in the hospital, he was well enough to be released. I heard that he had witnessed to every doctor and nurse in the hospital. After release, he went to San Carlos to let them know that he had recovered. When asked to give a testimony, he told the church, "I was really sick, and I told Pastor Carter that the next day I was going to be with the Lord. But Pastor Carter would not give me permission to die." The church got a good laugh out of that, and Brother Gerodias had to call me and tell me about it.

By Sunday, March 18, 1979, our attendance spiked to 261 and 14 accepted Christ as their own personal Savior. One hundred fifty-one of the 261 were adults. The adults could no longer be accommodated in the living room. We divided the preaching service with me preaching to one group in the house and the Filipino preacher preaching to the other group out in the yard.

The officials in charge of issuing building permits in Bacolod City were dragging their feet on giving us a building permit, probably in hopes of receiving some under the table money. At last they gave us a tentative building permit, but it still needed final approval. But they kept finding small things they wanted changed. We had been taking a building offering from our own people, plus the money that was being donated from supporting churches. We had $10,000 on hand to begin building.

In April, 1979, it was time for youth camp again. We scheduled it for the 23rd to the 27th and rented another beach resort. One of our ladies, Mrs. Malvas, had donated the runt out of a litter of pigs to the Lord. She said that after she donated the runt, it grew faster than all the other pigs and became the largest in the litter. By the time of our youth camp, the pig weighed almost 200 pounds. We rented a big road bus to carry everyone to the youth camp, and that big old pig was tied on the back of the bus. We slaughtered him at the youth camp, and he provided a lot of food for the group of about 150 campers.

At long last the city issued us our building permit. We worked from January until June before it was finally issued. The red tape was unbelievable. During June our old friend, Brother Ababon, who was our builder at San Carlos, came to oversee the construction. We also bought 25 tons of cement, 50 tons of steel, and two truckloads of lumber. Inflation had increased the cost while all the delay with a building permit was going on. We paid for all the materials and labor as we went along and I estimated that we still needed $18,000 to complete the project. In America, you could go to the bank and make a loan, but that option is not available in the Philippines. During this same month, Bacolod had an average attendance of 245 and there were 72 saved.

The church building had a framework of cement and steel. By September all the framework was finished and the floor joists were installed on the second floor where the auditorium would be. We purchased prebuilt roof trusses and they were in route. The metal roofing cost was $1,820.

On Thursday, October 4<sup>th</sup>, as I was working on the floor joists on the second floor, my stomach began to ache. I finally had to go back home and lie down. After a doctor was called in to examine me, I was rushed to the hospital with a ruptured appendix. As Harriett was checking me into the hospital with the paperwork, Jing-Jing Usaraga and Virgie Larida were pushing me to my room in a wheelchair when I passed out. I woke up with wind in my face as I was being pushed down the hall of the hospital at high speed. The two ladies were running and pushing me along in the wheelchair. I asked where they were going. They said they were taking me to the emergency room. I told them to turn around and take me to my room. It really scared those two ladies. They thought I had died, they said, "We thought, no more missionary." I fainted again as they were x-raying me. The doctor performed emergency surgery just before midnight.

After church services on Sunday morning, my hospital room filled with visitors from church. I counted 37 in there at one time. On Wednesday, the hospital would not release me, but they gave me a pass to leave the hospital to attend church. After church, it was back to my room in the hospital. I laughed and told our church that night, "Being in the hospital is no excuse for missing church."

After getting released from the hospital, I began shopping for windows for our building. The plans called for lots of windows as we needed a lot of air to cool the building when filled with people. The Philippine National Bank had recently remodeled and put in new windows. Their old windows were stacked out behind their bank. They had enough windows to do our entire church. I saved an enormous amount when I bought their used windows. We had to repair the hinges, latches, and install new glass, but it greatly reduced the cost. They were steel windows that opened up and let lots of air come in.

By the end of December when we tallied our results for the year, we found that the total souls saved in Bacolod and the mission churches was 769 and 154 baptized. Total combined attendance for all our churches and missions averaged 1,299.

To save the trip to the river to baptize new converts, we built an outside baptistry in the corner of our church lot. Now we just had to walk across the street to baptize. This was temporary as we were building an inside baptistry in our new building.

At the beginning of 1980, the main structure of our building was finished, but the finishing work took a tremendous amount of time. Money was short and every week I would spend all the money I had to make payroll. We kept praying, and somehow by the next payday, I would have money enough to pay the workers again. This happened week after week. Finally, the church was completely finished. We still had $3,000 of bills. I covered that out of my personal support until it came in. Now the church was paid off completely and had no debt! The very first service in the church, just before it was completed, was the wedding ceremony for one of our Bible women to a Filipino pastor. We used Bible women to visit women and the pastors to visit men. (Bible women is what Filipinos call women who are employed by the church to do visitation.) The last month we met in the house the average attendance was 221.

In April, 1980, to give our new church building a jump start, we planned a revival and invited Missionary Herb Hayes along with the Singing Hayes Family to be the speaker and to sing. Then we asked Brother Hayes to preach at our annual Youth Camp. There were 16 saved, 5 baptized, and 40 surrendered their lives to the Lord during the revival and youth camp. We also ordained two National pastors at the youth camp. Two of the 40 who surrendered their lives were the Dela Cruz brothers. They were from Manapla. His brother became a pastor in the Philippines and God called Lomer Dela Cruz to be a missionary in Cambodia. He has now been in Cambodia for 20 years and in his first 15 years started 21 churches. I asked Dr. Heng Lim, my good friend from Cambodia, if he knew Brother Dela Cruz, and he told me that he is now the president of the Bible college in Cambodia. Brother David Hardy met missionary Dela Cruz in California about five years ago. After learning he was from Negros island, he inquired if Brother Dela Cruz knew Barton Carter. He answered that Brother Carter was preaching a sermon called "God's Valiant Men" when he surrendered his life to the Lord.

Somewhere about this time, Missions Director Bob Baird and his wife Ann, visited our work. Brother Baird, seeing the close proximity of our rental home to the church, suggested that we apply for a home loan and buy our home. The loan was no problem, but it took a lot of haggling from the bank that owned the home. They wanted to just continue renting it to us. Finally, we were able to purchase the house and our loan payment to the Fellowship was $150 per month.

Adam Sennarillos, Phoebe's brother, had graduated from Bible college and agreed to come to Bacolod to become music director. He was very good with the music, but I learned a valuable lesson. Adam was from the Cebuano tribe and the people of Bacolod were from the Ilonggo tribe. They did not want to be directed by a Cebuano. It got bad enough that Adam eventually resigned. He kept preaching and later was murdered by the communist New People's Army.

In June, we launched on a new ministry. The Bacolod Bible Baptist Seminary was founded to train the young people on this island who had surrendered their lives to the Lord. We started with a dozen students. We converted some of the SS rooms to dormitory rooms. They had to supply and cook their own food, but they would have had to do that anyway if they were home. Some who lived in Bacolod could continue to live at home. They had to be a high school graduate to qualify. I started teaching eight to ten hours a week in the Bible college. I averaged speaking 13 to 15 times per week which included the 8 to 10 hours teaching at the college.

During this same time, the church in San Carlos City was flourishing under Pastor Eddie Gerodias. He reported that the offerings had doubled and in a special evangelistic Sunday there were 46 saved and seven baptized.

For our third anniversary at Bacolod, Missionary David Steffy was the special speaker. The attendance that day was 403 with eight saved and two baptized, and one joined by letter. Pastor Joel Duhina, one of the workers at Bacolod had been called to his home town of Dumangas, on the island of Panay. Bacolod Baptist Church voted to open up a new mission at Dumangas, and to send Pastor Duhina under our authority. Joel answered the call of God to go there, and the Bacolod Baptist answered the call of God to send him.

December was very special. Brother David Hardy, his wife Grace, his son Wayne, and Kathy Aldrich came on a mission trip and spent about a week with us. We all crowded into our little Toyota, three in front and three in back, and toured the mission churches. One mission we went to was a several hours walk up in the mountains at a place called Malatamban. When we got to the bamboo floored house, it was customary to remove your shoes before entering. I remember preaching there barefooted that day.

There were several to be baptized which required hiking two hours out of the mountains to get to the ocean. The church asked Brother Hardy to do the baptisms. It required wading out a good way from shore to get into deep enough water. Brother Hardy said, "Bart, if I'm going to get wet, you are too. I want you to wade out and take pictures." On Wednesday evening, we attended services at San Carlos and Brother Hardy preached.

The next day, we continued visiting churches until we came to Stop Ignaldo, a small community on the national highway where a dirt road wanders off into the mountains to San Isidro. We bought some cans of vienna sausage and beans as we were going to spend the night at the Villaflor home and did not want to come empty handed. It was about five miles. The road had many mudholes. The Toyota could not get through them loaded down, so I would have everyone get out, I would drive through the mudhole, everyone would get back in, and we would continue until we came to the next mudhole. This continued until we came to one mudhole the Toyota could not get through. We parked the Toyota and hiked through the mud about the last mile and a half. We were a sad looking bunch of Americans when we got there.

The Villaflors were very gracious. For supper they served us rice and vienna sausage. They gave up their bedrooms. Harriett and I got a bed. Next door Kathy and Grace had a bed, and in the next room Dave and Wayne had to sleep on the floor on *benigs*. The Villaflors slept in the hall. A Filipino bed has no mattress, just woven bamboo. There was very little difference than sleeping on the floor. In the next room, we overheard Kathy tell Grace, "My mother is never going to believe this." The next morning when we were served breakfast, again we were served rice and vienna sausage. I was so proud of the Hardys. They acted like they had vienna sausage and rice for breakfast every day. On the way home, we had to stop at a garage to have the skid plate repaired under the Toyota.

Saturday, they accompanied us along for the extension classes as we taught the children in the different barrios. They were on one team but there were several more teams working at the same time. Then on Sunday, Kathy played the piano, Wayne sang a special, and Brother Hardy preached. We had put on a big push as it was our Christmas service, and our attendance that day was 976.

Early in 1981, we had to repair the flooring on our house. Termites had attacked the joists of the house and you could see space between the walls and the floor. This only affected the three bedrooms as they were the only part of the house with wooden flooring. I was at a loss about what to do, but Filipinos knew what to do. They would go a room at a time, tear out the flooring, replace all the joists, and put in new hardwood flooring. They went right down the line, room by room, and made it like new again. The walls again went all the way and joined the floor. We just slept in different rooms while they were repairing our bedroom. We also had to put a new metal roof on the house.

About this same time a single missionary lady, Nancy Strong, came to Bacolod to help in the work there. She was an excellent pianist and started teaching in the Bible college. Jing-Jing was now also teaching accordion in the Bible college. Ruby Chua was teaching English and typing. Furlough time was coming up and reservations were made to fly to the States on April 8th. At this time Jing-Jing was working for the church full time and Ruby Chua was now my secretary. This furlough, she would be in charge of all the financial dealings while we were gone. I arranged with the bank for her to be able to sign checks on the church account and my account. Our Bacolod church supported missions. We supported one foreign missionary family and a lot of Philippine missions that she had to send support to each month. Just as Jing-Jing had done the term before, she did a good job and there was a good balance in the bank when we returned.

# Chapter 8 – **Second Furlough**

Harriett had been suffering from shoulder pain for some time. The Filipino doctors had been doctoring with pain medicine and nothing had been done for the cause. When we arrived in the States, we were going to visit all our children, but we only got as far as Houston to visit our daughter Kathy and her husband Larry Bice. As Harriett's pain was so severe, we took her to the doctor in Houston. They diagnosed her problem as a frozen shoulder and put her in the hospital for immediate surgery. While she was recovering in her hospital room, the hospital would not allow our grandchildren in the room to visit her. She was on a first-floor room. I took the kids around to the back of the hospital and found the window to her room. Then we opened the window, and they could visit with their grandmother through the window. After her release from the hospital, both of us had to take medicine to try to clear our bodies of amoeba. Harriett's shoulder surgery required a lot of painful rehab.

While we were in Houston, I used our son-in-law, Larry Bice's, airplane to get my biannual flight review so I could fly myself to some of our churches. The instructor had me climb up above scattered clouds to do all the required maneuvers. After completing them and still above the clouds, he pulled the throttle back to idle and asked me, "Where are you going to land?" I used the navigation radio to point me back toward the airport, and put the airplane in a glide. When I descended to the clouds, I found a hole and circled down through it. The airport was in sight. I entered the pattern on crosswind and landed the airplane on the runway without ever adding power. I passed the biannual.

Brother Hardy of Eastland Baptist had telephoned us in the Philippines and offered us the use of a new missionary apartment they had just built. We would be the first missionaries to use it. This trip home we needed nothing. There were sheets on the beds, towels in the linen closet, and even food in the pantry and the refrigerator. There were even steaks in the freezer. After getting settled in, we were able to buy an Oldsmobile 88 diesel automobile. This gave us a comfortable ride and 25 miles to the gallon performance as we reported God's blessings to our churches. It was the best of worlds, God had done all the work and all the blessing, and we got to report all those blessings to our churches. God had just used us. As Brother Eli Harju had taught us in Bible college, God can use the jawbone of an ass.

My son-in-law, Pastor Lowell Haggerty of Lake Milton Baptist Temple, had Harriett and I stay at their house while I reported to churches in Ohio. A branch of the Heritage Baptist University was there and I enrolled in correspondence courses and earned both my Bachelors in 1981 and Masters during 1982 on that furlough. I needed these degrees because of the founding of the Bacolod Bible Baptist Seminary.

One of the ladies in Lake Milton Baptist Temple sold Avon products and she had a customer that was a Filipina. She made an appointment for the pastor and I to visit her. She came from a different area than I in the Philippines, so I could not speak her dialect. We talked in English, but it was Filipino English. The accents are in different places which makes it sound very different. We spoke of things in the Philippines in general for a while and then we began to speak of spiritual things. She accepted Christ as her Savior and was saved. After we left, Brother Haggerty said, "Bart, I couldn't understand a word of what either one of you were saying."

Our daughter, Kathy, and her husband, Larry Bice, hosted the Carter Family reunion from June 18th through 20th. Mike lived in the vicinity so there were beds available at both homes. Then on

Sunday, the 21st, her pastor, Pastor David Burkholder of Bandera Street Baptist Church, had me as special speaker. If I am not mistaken it was Father's Day. At the invitation Sunday evening, my son-in-law, Larry Bice, rededicated his life to the Lord. He was a graduate of Bible Baptist College in Springfield, Missouri and had previously served as youth director in several churches. At the time, he was a police officer in Houston, Texas and also owned a sporting goods store, and was quickly becoming financially secure. He resigned from the police department and later became pastor of a church in Colorado, then Dumas, Texas, then Mineral Wells, Texas, and finally back to pastor in Houston until his death.

My memory of the furlough is a little hazy. Again, I crisscrossed the United States and preached at numerous churches and was in many mission conferences. This time I flew small aircraft to many of my appointments to save time. I saw the need for an instrument rating and began to take instrument instruction in August, 1981. My son-in-law, Larry Bice, loaned me his airplane, a Cherokee Warrior, to take the instrument instruction in. God had me sell my airplane years ago and now He was allowing me to fly again.

I picked up the airplane from the Baytown airport near Houston on September 25th, and flew it to Tulsa's Harvey Young airport which is near Eastland Baptist where Harriett and I were living in the mission apartment. Jerry Dixon was my instrument instructor. He had moved from Hawaii to Tulsa to become involved in the Fellowship Aviation Supply and Training that Tom Craft had founded. In November, by using the airplane I was able to be in two mission conferences the same week, one in Denver and the other in Cape Girardeau, Missouri.

Harriett and I flew to the Denver mission conference VFR (visual flight rules) but the trip to Cape Girardeau had to be on instruments. We flew back to Tulsa and picked up Jerry Dixon, my instrument flight instructor, to make the IFR (instrument flight rules) trip to Cape Girardeau. Night overtook us before we arrived in Cape Girardeau. Flying in clouds at night is like flying in a bottle of ink. I enjoyed the challenge, but Harriett did not like it a bit. Later she told Brother Hardy, "When we came down out of the clouds, the lights of the runway were right there in front of us." Brother Hardy told her, "If they hadn't been there, that would be the time to worry."

I returned the airplane to Pastor Larry Bice by meeting him and his family in Fort Collins, Colorado in January 1982. I received my instrument rating April 19, 1982, shortly before returning to the Philippines on our third term.

Shortly before our departure from Tulsa, Eastland Baptist Church gave me a check for $10,000 to buy a new vehicle when we returned to the Philippines. Also, on the 16th of May, 1982, Brother Hardy led the church in a commissioning ceremony for missionary service, making Eastland Baptist Church my sending church.

Harriett and I stopped in El Paso, Texas to see my parents as we were going to the west coast. I was able to buy eight or ten good used accordions at a pawn shop. Filipinos were very good musicians and these accordions were the main instrument in the missions and young churches. We had already acquired about 20 mechanical typewriters from the Tulsa School District to use in our college. We were going to be better equipped than ever before for our ministry. All our college graduates would be proficient on a typewriter.

## Chapter 9 – **Philippines Third Term**

We returned home to the Philippines in June, 1982. After a short layover in Manila we caught a flight to Bacolod. Bacolod City has a nice airport. This time we flew from Manila to Bacolod City on a Philippine Airline jet and were met with a large group of members from the Bible Baptist Church of Bacolod City. I had left Pastor Boy Arzaga as pastor while I was in the States. He announced, "When that airplane's wheels touched the ground, you became pastor again."

A question that is often asked is, "Can a missionary be a pastor or does he operate as only a missionary?" My answer is he can be both. The missionary must be in authority until the National is fully trained. Also, a missionary must have a pastor's heart to pastor people. He has an inner need to pastor a congregation. In addition, he is also helping start churches as a missionary.

In Bacolod, I tried to have Monday as my day off. I did not schedule any teaching in the Bible College on Monday, but I seldom had that day free. My pastors knew that I was free that day so there was a constant stream of them through my office on Mondays. They came to ask advice and for fellowship.

The third year of the Bible college started soon after our return to the field with 37 full time students. The Sunday school rooms we had converted to dormitories were overflowing. We needed a dormitory and college building. We began to look for property to put the building on and found property back to back with our church.

We began searching for a good missionary vehicle to purchase with the $10,000 Eastland Baptist Church had given us. We decided on a Toyota Land Cruiser, a four-wheel drive with a high clearance to get through muddy roads, and were able to buy a new one. It was made in the Philippines and was made for Philippine roads.

Our new vehicle made visiting the other missions and churches on Negros much easier. We still used the pickup for heavy loads and when many people needed to be transported, but it was getting in pretty bad shape. It was just getting worn out. It very seldom made a trip in which it was not overloaded.

The anniversary for the Bacolod church is the first Sunday in September each year, but we decided to celebrate it on the last Sunday in 1982. We invited Missionary Delbert Hooge to be our special speaker and set a goal for attendance of 500 and a goal of 20 to be saved. Brother Hooge is a second-generation missionary as he is the son of Missionary Frank Hooge. He learned to speak in the Philippine language playing with Filipino kids while he was growing up.

Two things are important in the Philippines for a missionary to keep operating at capacity: the daily siesta and the yearly vacation. Another Baptist missionary organization had some cabins in Baguio City for their missionaries. It was called Doanes Rest. We could rent a cabin in the off season when their missionaries were not there. The elevation at Baguio City was about the same as Denver, Colorado. They are both mile high cities. Living at sea level in the tropics, going to the mountains and where it was cooler was wonderful. The cabins were stocked with beds, sheets, towels, and a working kitchen. There was even a fireplace. We would buy wood, build a fire in the fireplace, and leave the windows and doors open so it wouldn't get too hot, and then set around by the fire.

One year, the Waters family and the Carter family rented adjoining cabins for our vacations. On church days we attended the church that Missionary Damon Woods pastored. The Woods family had been to the States on furlough and they were returning while we were in Baguio on our vacation. The church was giving a party to celebrate the return of their missionary and they invited us to attend. There was to be a meal, and in Baguio dog meat is a delicacy. It cost more in the market than beef. Brother Waters asked me if we were going to the party. I told him that we were. He said, "You know they will be serving dog meat. Are you going to eat it?" I told him we were going to eat enough to be polite. He said, "If you are going, we are also."

That evening we were at the church welcoming the Woods family home. The food was going to be buffet style so you could take what you wanted. We were planning on getting just a small amount, but Brother Woods said, "You visitors just sit where you are at. Our people will bring your plates of food to you." Instead of a small helping, our plates were heaped up. They had made seven different dishes out of the dog meat. Harriett told me later, "I prayed every time I took a bite." Earlier, Harriett had ordered a hamburger at a restaurant in Baguio City and told me it tasted "different." After eating at the church, she realized that the hamburger she had eaten was actually a dogburger.

In 1982, we went to Baguio City for vacation in the fall of the year, from the middle of October to the beginning of November. The Filipino pastors did all the preaching and taught my seminary classes for me.

Christmas Eve was on a Friday in 1982. I was invited to San Isidro to preach for them for a 10am service. Then we drove about four hours going back to Bacolod for the Watch Night service. The results during 1982 at Bible Baptist Church of Bacolod was an average attendance of 191 and with 355 saved. Our other works combined reported 649 saved for a total of 1,004 saved. The average combined total attendance for our other works that reported was 1,494. (We did not always get a report from everyone.)

Time seemed to go by so swiftly. The church in San Carlos City was now ten years old. We started with the first services in January 1973 and now it was 1983. We were asked to come and help them celebrate. Brother Eddie Gerodias was such a good pastor. They were outgrowing their building. In the anniversary service there were 15 to 20 saved. What blessed our hearts was to see so many of those saved in the very first service still there, faithful in church. A reporter came from the San Carlos newspaper and wrote:

*"The Bible Baptist Church located at San Julio Subdivision celebrated its 10th anniversary last Sunday, January 9th. The occasion was attended by the founder the Rev. Barton Carter, who came with Mrs. Carter from Bacolod City. With them were Rev. and Mrs. Ed Butler, American missionaries assigned to Roxas City. There was an overflowing crowd, which even spilled out to the street fronting the church.*

*In the evening, a film "The Burning Hell" was shown to the crowd. It depicted a life of torture for all eternity to people whose wickedness in life while living, is punishable in the burning hell.*

*Rev. Eddie Gerodias is the Pastor of the Bible Baptist Church."*

Bacolod Bible Baptist Seminary was running smoothly. The typewriters we had bought from Tulsa School District had no letters on the keys. They were made for students to learn touch typing. One of our young people was an artist. He made a big picture of a keyboard with the correct letters and numbers on it. We placed it in front of the class just in case they forgot. We had Typing I and

Typing II, so each student had two years of typing lessons before graduating.

English is the language of education in the Philippines, so we taught three years of English. I was teaching a course in bookkeeping and accounting when I discovered a shortcoming in the Philippine school system's math. In the Philippine schools, students are not required to memorize the multiplication tables. None of the accounting was coming out because of mistakes in math. I had to teach the students the multiplication table and the problem was solved.

The Philippines was becoming dangerous because of the communist party and the National People's Army. There were ambushes where military vehicles were ambushed and soldiers killed. There were busses stopped by barricades and all the passengers robbed. It reminded me of stage coach robberies I had read about in the wild west days. We were told that every time we went into the mountains there was a "gun at our head." Mostly we just ignored the warnings and kept on doing what we had been doing all the time we were in the Philippines.

Late in January, 1983, the American Consul and Embassy officers came to talk to missionaries about making plans as to how to exit the Philippines in an emergency. The governor of the Island of Negros hosted the event at the governor's palace. He provided space and privacy so the Embassy officials could tell the missionaries what they needed to know to be able to leave on a moment's notice. The Governor also provided a catered meal for everyone.

Meanwhile, the ministry went forward as usual. The first Sunday evening in February, the film, "The Burning Hell" was shown to a crowd of about 1,000 in the Bacolod church. Fifty-one responded to the invitation and received Christ as their Savior. From Monday through the next Sunday there was an evangelistic meeting with Rev. Eddie Gerodias as the evangelist. Thirty-three more were saved during the evangelistic meeting. For the month of February there were 119 saved.

In the middle of February, Bible Baptist Church of Bacolod City ordained its two pastors and one mission pastor. We were preparing them so that if we were to have to leave they would be fully prepared. We were in the process of buying property for the dormitory for the Bible College and had contracted an architect to prepare the plans.

After eleven years of hard use on the primitive Philippine roads, our old Dodge pickup just wore out. I had already replaced the Dodge engine and transmission with a surplus Toyota engine and transmission, but too many other things were wrong. I just junked it out.

In front, and across the street, from one of the member's house, I saw the chassis of an old WWII jeep that had been left by the American GIs after the war. It had been lengthened and changed into a jeepney and used until the engine wore out. It was a Ford jeep and had to be over 40 years old. There was no engine, transmission, or wheels left on it. Just the chassis laying there.

I bought the chassis, had a machine shop cut it in two, and added two more feet in length. Then we took the Toyota engine and transmission that had been in the pickup, and installed them in the jeepney. Then we installed a Toyota Hilux rear end and differential, put on wheels and tires, and installed new padded benches for people to sit on. It looked like a wreck looking for a place to happen, but it ran well, and could handle 25 to 27 passengers inside, not counting those standing on the rear bumper. It was a people mover. This was the bus of our bus ministry. We just called it the jeepney ministry.

On March 24th, Bacolod Bible Baptist Seminary held its first Commencement exercise to graduate the first class of students. Rev. Woody Sherrill, pastor of Trinity Baptist Church of Austin, Texas was the speaker. It was a thrill to watch as those students we had worked with for three years, walked across that stage and received their diplomas. We also gave each graduating student some important books they would need to start a library of books.

On June 7th, the Bible college started its new year with 37 full time students. Brother Ababon was back overseeing the construction of the college dormitory. It would have bedrooms and baths for both male and female students, a kitchen, and several classrooms.

In the first four months of 1983, Bacolod's result was 195 saved and 43 baptized. The churches and missions on Negros had increased to 35 works, and I had challenged the National pastors with a goal of 100 churches for our island. The other churches reported another 240 saved and 47 baptized during those four months. At the time I estimated that if that rate was maintained, by the end of the year there would be 1,100 saved and 227 baptized on Negros.

In July, God permitted us to see our ministry go full cycle. The church at San Carlos was started with 44 being saved on the first weekend. The pastor at San Carlos won a young man to the Lord who surrendered for full-time service. He sent this young man to our Bible college in Bacolod where he graduated that March. He in turn started a new work in Gihulngan on July 24th, as a mission out of the San Carlos church. On his first service, he had 90 in attendance and, just like in San Carlos years ago, 44 people got saved. He used an old tobacco warehouse for a meeting place, and I sat on a bale of tobacco to listen as he preached.

Although we did not know it yet, out days in the Philippines were coming to an end. Thelma Mahilum, one of the ladies that had allowed us to start the church in San Carlos in their living room, was murdered at Malatamban. This was one of the areas Brother Hardy had visited while he was there. The Malatamban folks had built a building, Thelma had gone there preparing for an evangelistic service when the National People's Army abducted her, beat her, and killed her by stabbing her to death. There were seventeen stab wounds. The pastor from there was able to escape, but the church in Malatamban was now closed.

The political party in opposition to the Marcos regime were holding political rallies because of the assassination of Aquino, and were creating an anti-American feeling across the Philippines. They wanted the Americans out. There was even rebellion in the church in Bacolod and vicious rumors were started. The dormitory was finished and paid for and our intentions were to turn the work on Negros over to the Nationals, return to the States to regroup, and then start over in a different area of the Philippines. A missionary must always build his work on the Lord so the work can continue after he is gone.

With the help of two missionary families, the Ed Butler and the Herb Hayes family, we sold the things we no longer needed, and crated up the things we did for shipping to the States. After a few days with the Hayes family in Baguio City, we took an early furlough and flew back to the States on December 5th. We returned to Tulsa, Oklahoma where Eastland Baptist Church, our sending church, is located.

# Chapter 10 – **Third Furlough**

Eastland Baptist Church's mission apartment was in use by another missionary on furlough so we rented an apartment. As we were uncrating our things and putting them in our apartment, my daughter, Sandra, and her daughter, Renee, were helping us. We had unpacked a picture frame with the picture removed. We just hung it on the wall until we found the picture that went in it. Sandra told her daughter, "Did I ever tell you about my invisible uncle?" Renee answered, "Oh Mother, you do not have an invisible uncle. There is no such thing." Sandra said, "Yes there is. See, here is his picture." You should have seen Renee's face when she saw the blank picture.

Our hearts were still in the Philippines and we were keeping in close contact with our National pastors and friends there. They were continuing in the work and still remembered our goal of 100 churches for the island of Negros. The church at Escalante was able to purchase property on which to build a new church.

The Fellowship Aviation Supply and Training, a ministry based out of Eastland Baptist Church, now owned two airplanes to be used by missionaries and for training. One was a Beechcraft Sundowner and the other a Maule M5. Brother Don Stroud was flight instructor and he gave me my biannual flight review and instrument competency check so that I was proficient to fly the airplanes.

On February 24th, Harriett and I flew the Maule to Fort Collins, Colorado to report to Bethel Baptist Church. From Fort Collins we flew to Great Falls, Montana, to be with Pastor Ron Roach and the Great Falls Baptist Temple for a week. On March 5th, we flew to Dumas, Texas to visit with my daughter, Kathy, and my son-in-law Pastor Larry Bice. From there we flew to Albuquerque, New Mexico to be in a meeting at Berean Baptist Church. During the month of March, we traveled 6,000 miles, saw eight souls saved, several surrendering their lives, and saw over $100,000 raised in the different mission conferences.

News from the Philippines was exciting. Another of our Bible college graduates started a new work at a place called Vallehermosa and construction had begun on the church building in Escalante.

Not all the news was so exciting. Pastor Eddie Gerodias wrote, "In San Carlos, killing has become so rampant, dead corpses are sometimes found floating in the sea. The work in Malatamban is still closed. We attempted to reopen it but another casualty fell, though not a member of the church, but the tension is still there."

A few months later the news was a little better. It seemed the Philippines had passed the crisis stage in their politics, and the government was stronger than it had been. A letter from one of my pastors informed me that since we had been in the States on furlough, four new churches had been started.

In about November, Dr. Philips, missionary to the Navajo Indians started trying to contact me. The Baptist Bible Navajo Church at Crystal, New Mexico was open with no one to pastor it. God had laid on his heart to ask me to change my field of service from the Philippine Islands to the Navajo Indians. He called Rev. Ronny Roach in Montana to try to locate me. Ronny told him he thought I was at my father's house in El Paso, Texas. He was able to contact me there.

I had started my deputation at his church on the Reservation, and when he asked me to consider changing my field there, I really did not feel like going there. I thought, just about anywhere but there. But I gave him a pious answer. I told him I would pray about it. I told Harriett what he had asked, and true to our word, we prayed about it. Harriett and I prayed about it overnight. When I prayed, the Lord laid the Navajo people on my heart. The next morning, I told Harriett that I felt like God wanted us on the Navajo Reservation. She told me that she got the same answer. I called Pastor David Hardy and discussed this change of field with him. It was decided that Pastor Hardy, myself, and Pancho Krebs would fly out to the Reservation on a survey trip. We made the survey trip on November 20th, and the Crystal church had a special Tuesday evening service so I could preach to them. God put His stamp of approval on the field change. After returning to Tulsa, we contacted Missions Director, Brother Carl Boonstra and requested a change of field.

## Chapter 11 – **The Navajo Reservation**

Our change of field request was brought before the Mission Committee at the February Fellowship meeting in California. Our approval was on February 18th and on March 4th, 1985, we left Tulsa for the Reservation. On the 9th, we had a used mobile home moved on to the mission site lease, and on the 10th, we had our first service. On the 20th, we brought the Maule airplane to use on the Reservation. The Fellowship Aviation Supply and Training had agreed to let us use the airplane in our Reservation ministry as long as we kept it insured and paid all the expenses. By the 24th the attendance reached 52.

In the middle of April, we used the Maule to visit churches in Dumas, Borger, and Perryton in the Texas panhandle. This would have been impossible if we had to use ground transportation.

So much is different from the Philippines and surprisingly, much is the same. In the Philippines, we were about 6 feet above sea level, on the Reservation at Crystal, the elevation is 7,800', a mile and a half above sea level. In the Philippines, we lived in the tropics with the temperature rarely dropping below 75 degrees. In Crystal, there are only three months out of the year that the temperature does not drop below freezing. In the Philippines, there is mass humanity, people everywhere. On the Reservation, people are thinly scattered, living in family camps. As to being the same, both need a Savior, and both respond to someone who truly loves them. Both the Filipinos and the Navajos earned a place in my heart.

The pastors in the Philippines were still doing the job. Several were in building programs and all were reporting souls saved. Jun Bastillo, one of the last graduates of the Bible college started a church since the beginning of 1985. He had been working with another pastor before this. His request to me was to help him pray for a wife, and he told me just the one he wanted. He remembered that I taught in Bible college to be specific in your prayers.

After I came to the Reservation, I preached several weeks before anyone came forward. I think they just did not know what to do. Finally, someone came forward and got saved, and in the next two services six more were saved. On Easter Sunday the attendance was 75!

In June, we had been on the Reservation three months and had seen 42 Navajos accept Jesus as Savior and we had baptized seven. Pastor Roach from Great Falls, Montana, owned a revival tent, and in June, brought it to the Reservation and held six weeks of tent revivals. One was at Dr. Philips church at Crownpoint, New Mexico. The revival at Crystal started on June 23$^{rd}$. The revival was a tremendous success. Navajos like tent revivals. The high attendance during the revival was 102, with 22 saved, and I baptized 17 out of the 22.

On one of the nights of the revival, one of my members introduced me to David Lee, one of his co-workers from the Chapter House, that he had invited to the revival meeting. Then he told me, "Pastor, I promised him that if he would come to the revival that you would take him home." He lived about 12 miles away over some terrible dirt roads. I agreed to take him home, and as we were on the way he told me, "Reverend Carter, I am an untamable drunk. Many men have tried to tame me and I cannot be tamed."

Making that statement to a missionary is like waving a red flag in front of a bull, I had to respond. I told David, "I know someone who can tame you." He said, "Who can tame me?" I told him, "Jesus can tame you. Let me show you." I pulled the car over to the side of the road, opened my Bible to the plan of salvation, and introduced him to the One that can tame untamable drunks. David

Lee got saved right there in the front seat of my car. God took away David's addiction to alcohol right then and he never took another drink. At the time David got saved he was 47 years old, did not have a wife or a driver's license, and was living with his father who was a medicine man.

He was faithful to come to church and would try to do anything I asked him to do. I even asked him to lead the singing one time, but that didn't work. He couldn't carry a tune in a bucket. A few months later, his mother died and he asked me to preach her funeral. He brought six nieces and nephews to church and they were saved also. Some of his brothers came from Idaho to the funeral. After the funeral was over, David went to Idaho with them to work in the potato harvest. I had made copies of my Sunday School lessons so each person in the class could have a copy. David took his copies with him and taught them to his relatives there in Idaho, then called me to send him more lessons. He had already taught all the lessons I had given him.

A few years later, David was working for Four Corners Power Company, had a driver's license, had married a wife, and adopted a daughter. Every time he came to the Reservation, he would always come to visit with me. He is an example of God's redemptive power. He is proof that God can tame the untamable.

During July, we held our very first Daily Vacation Bible School for the Navajo children in our area. Our daughter, Kathy Bice, came from her husband's church in Dumas, Texas to help with the DVBS. Five of the children were saved and four were baptized the following Sunday. The fifth one wanted to be baptized but her mother would not give permission.

While Brother Roach was at Crystal, he helped skirt the mobile home to winterize it, and Dennis Bynam came from Eastland Baptist in Tulsa, and installed a chain link fence around our mobile home. We insulated the church and Brother Ed Chapman installed two propane furnaces, and put in new duct work in our church, and would not take a penny in payment. He donated both labor and material.

The Bureau of Indian Affairs boarding school was only about 100 yards from our church site. When school started in September, we were allowed to teach religion one hour a week to the Navajo students from families that were of similar faith. I was amazed. In the United States of America, I was able to teach, give an invitation, and lead children to Christ right in the school. We were able to continue these classes all the years we were on the Reservation.

It soon became apparent we needed four-wheel drive to get over the Reservation roads. My Dad found a Chevrolet Suburban for me in El Paso and brought it to the Reservation. I bought another at a government surplus auction. These two Suburbans were what we used to bring people to church. That was our bus ministry. I drove one and Harriett drove the other. We packed the Navajos in Filipino style and would often have over 20 in a nine passenger Suburban. Sometimes when the Suburbans got to church it was hard to tell what color they were. If the roads were not icy and snowbound, they were muddy. And I mean axle deep mud. Sometimes the Suburbans looked like mud balls going down the road.

One very cold and icy Sunday morning, Harriett and I went on our separate routes to pick up people for the church services. The Surburban Harriett was driving developed a problem. After it was running and in gear, when you stepped on the accelerator to start moving, the engine would just die. Usually, if you just restarted the engine, you could get it to go. Harriett got about ¼ mile from the church and stopped at a stop sign. She tried time and again to get the Suburban to move again. Every time she stepped on the accelerator, the engine would just die. Finally, she decided to walk back to the church. Dressed for church and with dress shoes on, she gathered all her teaching materials and started walking back to the church on the icy road. The temperature was below freezing. About half way back to the church, she came to a very slick spot and her feet went out from under her. She crashed to the ground and her teaching material and Bible went everywhere. Needless to say, she was not in a good mood when I got back to church.

Our years in the Philippine Island helped prepare us for being missionaries to the Navajo people. We were used to working cross culturally. Different cultures think in a different way. A missionary should not expect a people from a different culture to think like an Anglo. Even different language groups in the Philippines had different cultures, as we had found out when we moved from people who spoke Cebuano to people who spoke Ilonggo.

Our job was not to teach American culture, either in the Philippines or on the Navajo Reservation. Neither did I go to either mission field to teach my thoughts on things. It was not important what I thought about anything. Our job as missionaries was to tell what God said in His Holy Bible. God's Word is truth and works everywhere in the world. God's Word touches and changes hearts.

Even with two new furnaces in our church, we still needed to gather wood for a wood stove in the church to help with the cost of propane. Every fall, we went into the Navajo Forest and gathered wood to use both in the church and in our mobile home. Because of the extreme cold, we had to gather about 10 cords of firewood each year. This involved lots of work. If a tree was dead in the Navajo Forest, residents of the Reservation could cut down that tree and use it for firewood. I would take one of our Navajo members to help, and we would find a dead tree that we could get close to with a suburban and a trailer. Usually we could find a dead pine tree that was about 65 feet tall and about 36 inches across. As a boy, my Dad had taught me how to notch a tree so that it would fall where you wanted it to. With a chain saw I would fell the tree. After it was lying on the ground, I would first use the chain saw to cut all the limbs off the trunk of the tree. Next, as I would use the chain saw to cut the trunk of the tree into about 16-inch lengths, The Navajo would start cutting the limbs into stove size lengths with an axe. Then he would debark the big lengths from the trunk of the tree. The reason the trunk of the tree had to be cut into about 16-inch lengths was because of weight. They were heavy enough that it took two men to lift one into the trailer. One tree took two loads on a tandem axle trailer to haul to the mission site lease. Total weight of the two loads was about two tons.

After the wood was back at the church site, the work had just started. First the tree had to dry out a couple of months. Then the wood had to be split into small enough firewood to fit into the stove or fireplace. When both Brother Dave Hardy and Brother Wayne Hardy came to the Reservation, they got to split some wood. I remember Wayne telling his Dad, "Look, I am making 4 by 4s."

One big problem on the Navajo Reservation is alcoholism. It may be the Native American genes that make the Navajo people so susceptible to strong drink. Every year we would hear of Navajos who were inebriated and had passed out or went to sleep in the extreme cold weather and then froze to death. The David Lee, that I told of earlier, had a near-death experience by going to sleep in a gully in cold weather. Fortunately, he was found by someone and taken to a hospital where they nursed him back to life.

One very cold Sunday evening as I was preaching, a very intoxicated man staggered in the door of our church and sat down close to the back of the church near the roaring wood fire. The temperature outside was about zero degrees. He sat down near one of our elderly Navajo ladies. I could see her nose twitch as she smelled the alcohol, then she got up and moved. I just kept preaching, and in a few minutes, he was already asleep on the pew. I knew who the man was. His name was Raymond, as his mother and his eight-year old son came to our church.

After the service was over and everyone was going home, I decided just to cover him with a blanket, leave the heat up on the furnaces, and let him sleep off his drunken stupor right there in the church. I still had a Suburban load of people to take home. After taking all our people home, I was driving back to the mission site lease with about six inches of fresh snow on the ground, when I saw the drunk man's eight-year old son standing alongside the road crying. I stopped and asked the boy what was wrong. He said, "Grandmother sent me to look for my dad, and I can't find him." I told him to get in the Suburban because his dad was at the church and I would take him to him.

When we arrived at the church, he started trying to wake his dad up but could not. I told him that the church was warm and just for both of them to sleep there until his dad woke up. He said, "No, I have to take him home. Grandmother will be worried." I decided I would try to take them home, but first I would have to wake him up to get him in the vehicle. I went into the kitchen and got a bath towel and got it sopping wet with ice cold water. When I put it on his face his eyes popped open, but nobody was home. I kept washing his face until finally he began to come around. With the help of Harriett and his son, we finally got him into the Suburban. I had the son sit right by him so he could not lie down and we started the several miles journey up in the mountain to their family camp. I left the window open where he was sitting so he would not get sleepy. When we arrived at their family camp, his son walked him into the *hogan* (traditional Navajo dwelling) where the grandmother was waiting.

A few days later, I saw Raymond at the Crystal boarding school, and was able to talk to him. I asked him if he had not been able to get to our church what would have happened. He agreed that he had come very close to freezing to death that night. Then I asked him about his eternal destiny if he had died. The next time we had service, Raymond came and received Christ as his Savior. He was still an alcoholic but he was a saved alcoholic.

We began to make plans to build an addition on to our church building as we had to put out folding chairs in addition to the pews every Sunday morning. From our first service on March 10$^{th}$ until the end of the year, God saved 80 Navajos and 33 were baptized. We were still working with the Philippine missions. Out of our work support, we helped them in building churches, making pews, and with some financial support. The pastors there were working under extreme difficulties, but they were getting the job done. At the time, I estimated between 500 and 600 saved in our works in the Philippines for the year.

By the end of January, 1986, we found out how cold it could get when you live and work a mile and a half above sea level. The average morning temperature at Crystal in January was minus 10 degrees. In February, the entire church was affected by sickness, and half of our people were sick. Harriett and I were also affected. We both got the flu and were bedridden for about three weeks. One of our very old couples took pneumonia which caused them to have to give up living alone. The man was put in a rest home and the woman went to live with her daughter.

After Pastor Ronny Roach had conducted the revival services on the Reservation last summer, he donated the revival tent to the missionaries to use. The missionaries set up the tent at a camping site in the mountains and began a Navajo Youth Camp. This was a very primitive camp with no facilities except what we prepared. But we ran into difficulties. Although permission had been given almost a year previously by the one who held the grazing rights to that place, some other Navajos (who were thought to be of the Peyote cult) told us we would have to move. To prevent hard feelings, we struck the tent on Wednesday and moved it back to the mission site lease in Crystal. We had tents set up all over the place. We still had the victory with five young people getting saved.

We had two of our grandchildren visiting with us and going to the youth camp with us. Our son Mike's children, Jacob and Jennifer, had come to the Reservation for a couple of weeks to visit. The Sunday night after the youth camp week, Jacob came to the altar during the invitation. When I spoke to him, he said, "Pawpaw, I don't think I am saved." He then got saved, and with his parents' permission, I baptized him the next Sunday.

We used the revival tent almost every year to conduct a tent revival at Crystal. The BIA boarding school would loan us a portable stage and folding chairs to seat the people. One year our speaker was Brother Roy Hawthorn, a Navajo Code Talker, from WWII. Our flyer read, "Come hear one of our own warriors tell you how to get saved." One of the ones who came to the revival was a Japanese reporter who wanted to hear and interview a code talker.

We needed extra space and I bought a used 10' X 50' mobile home and moved it to our mission site. It housed my office and was a place to prepare sermons and lessons.

One problem for a missionary on the Navajo Indian Reservation is winning the trust of the people. The Navajo have been cheated so many times by Anglos that there is a strong distrust. The white man has and is still lying to and cheating the Navajo people. Here are a couple of examples:

A Singer sewing machine salesman came onto the Reservation and sold a sewing machine to the wife of Dr. Philips' Navajo preacher. He neglected to tell her it was an electric model. There was not an electric line within 15 miles of her house. When her husband came home, he took the sewing machine, went to Dr. Philips for help, and they tried to return the sewing machine to the Singer company in Gallup. They would not take the sewing machine back and said they had already sold the note to a loan company. I never found out how that problem was resolved.

One of the members of the church in Crystal was also cheated. He had been paid for property that the United States Congress had decreed that he had to sell because it was inside the Hopi Reservation. He went to Flagstaff, Arizona and ordered a new automobile. It was to come from the factory equipped as he had ordered. He paid for the new car in full. He kept going to the dealership and asking if his car had come in yet. They kept telling him it hadn't arrived. Then, he found out by accident the car had come in and was being used as part of the rental fleet. His wife sat in my living room telling me about it and said, "He thought we were just dumb Indians." They pressed charges and the man responsible ended up going to prison, and my member got his money returned to him.  Needless to say, he did not buy another vehicle from that dealership.

I even heard of someone trying to get a lease to set up a mission, when they were not going to set up a mission at all, but were trying to set up a place where they could sell liquor.

Something that makes mission work difficult on the Navajo Reservation is that the land is all owned by the Navajo Tribe and not by individual Navajo people.  The Navajo people then have home site leases, grazing right leases, and a church must have a mission site lease.  When God calls a preacher from among the Navajo people, he cannot just go to some other area and start a church.  He has no home site lease at the other area.  While at Crystal, God called Raymond Mullahom to preach.  I trained him and eventually led the church at Crystal to call him as pastor.

During the winter of 1986 – 1987, the weather was brutal.  There were times when we were snowed in.  The snow started piling up in November and didn't melt until late in March.  One Sunday, the temperature was 25 below zero.  Only one of the Suburbans would start, but we still had a good attendance.  All of March the church was jam packed and there were people at the altar almost every service.  We made plans to build an addition on to the church making an L-shaped Sunday School and Fellowship Hall.  The Navajos started a building fund and were setting money aside for this needed addition.  God touched the heart of the folks at Park Hill Baptist Church in Pueblo, Colorado to be a sister church to the Navajo Bible Baptist Church of Crystal.  This turned out to be a blessing to both churches.  Their youth director was a skilled carpenter and they made plans to come and frame up the new addition.

In February, I started working on getting my pilot instructors license.  On April 24, 1987, I became a Certified Flight Instructor.

My plan was to teach other missionaries to be pilots but instead it was helpful in reaching Navajo officials in government. I taught the assistant attorney general of the tribe to fly. I taught one of the attorneys in his office how to fly. And, I taught the tribes' Financial officer how to fly. One of the ways it helped was when the tribe was talking about legalizing liquor sales on the Reservation, the legal department came to me and asked for advice. I advised against it and gave them a book detailing the governmental costs associated with alcoholism. The costs would easily surpass any taxes they got from alcohol sales. Legalizing liquor was rejected.

By this time, I had been using the Maule in the mission work for three years. When I tried to insure it for giving flight instruction the cost of the insurance was prohibitive. I returned the Maule to the FAST Ministry for others to use, and bought a Cherokee 180. The Cherokee could be insured for flight training for 1/3 the price for the same type of insurance on the Maule. It had been 24 years since God told me to sell my airplane. Now He allowed me to own one again. It would also turn out to be a good investment.

The second week in June we held a Daily Vacation Bible School. We had a great attendance with nine young people getting saved. One day, as Harriett was overseeing the craft time, one of the young boys took some of the paint they were using in their project and painted war paint on his face. Harriett was so shocked but the adult Navajos thought it was hilarious. One of their young people was on the war path. Luckily it was water dissolvable and washed off easily.

Our church had already laid the foundation of the new addition so that it was ready for the Park Hill Baptist young people to come and frame out. We insulated it well, under the floor, over the ceiling, and the outside walls. We installed wall heaters so it would be comfortable. Our daughter, Gloria, and her husband, Pastor Lowell Haggerty, from Lake Milton Baptist Temple in Ohio came for a visit, and Lowell helped tile the floor and stucco the ceiling and put on the finishing touches to our new Fellowship Hall. Berean Baptist Church in Albuquerque gave us a folding wall that we installed, making two Sunday School rooms when it was closed and one large Fellowship Hall when it was open.

About the middle of January, 1988, I was teaching Bible at the BIA boarding school near our house. I taught a salvation message and then gave an invitation. Nineteen Navajo students received Christ as their Savior. There is an advantage of the Navajo Nation being a nation within a nation.

On June 15, 1988, Harriett's dear sweet mother went to be with the Lord. She lived to be 93 years old. I asked my son-in-law Pastor Larry Bice to preach the funeral. We gave thanks that we were not still laboring in the Philippines. If we had been in the Philippines, we could not have attended the funeral.

June was a busy time. The week of the 20th was Daily Vacation Bible school and the next week, Park Hill Baptist Church of Pueblo, Colorado came and installed a new roof on our church. Marvin Long was my associate pastor then and he preached when I was off the Reservation trying to raise extra support.

In October, 1988, Harriett and I flew the Cherokee 180 to El Paso to visit my aging parents for a few days. While there, I went with my dad to his appointment with his heart doctor. While there, I began to feel faint and had to lie down. Eventually I was transported by ambulance to the Emergency Room. They found my kidneys had locked down and I had to have prostrate surgery. After the surgery, the doctor told me that I could not drive for 30 days. I asked him if I could fly and he said, "Sure." I thought, at least I can get home. But Daddy told the doctor I was going to fly my own airplane. The next time the doctor came in he told me, "And you can't fly an airplane for 30 days also." Harriett and I spent the next 30 days visiting with my folks in El Paso.

The old saying goes, "You never miss the water until the well runs dry." The main water line coming to our church froze early in January, 1989, and it was several months before we were able to have running water again. We hauled our water in 5-gallon cans from mostly the Chapter House. The Chapter House is the local Navajo form of government. Maybe it would be the equivalent of a court house.

We had now been living in Crystal almost four years, and the Navajos had learned that they could come to us when they were in trouble. One night, in the extremely cold weather, a Navajo man woke Harriett and I up at 4am. He was almost frozen to death, and wanted a place to come in out of the cold. Harriett made a pot of coffee and then she began to cook sausage and eggs. After a hot meal, he listened while I told him the Gospel story. Not only was his life saved that morning, his soul was saved also.

Our Suburban was worn out. It already had over 60,000 miles on it when we bought it. We had put another 40,000 miles on it on the unimproved roads, and most of the time using four-wheel drive. After trying to buy another Suburban and never having enough money to get one, we decided to rebuild the one we had. Harriett followed me in our car as I drove it to Gallup, New Mexico to the Chevrolet dealership. It would barely make it up the hills and when I finally got there, they had me shut off the engine. That was it. It would not start again. They had to push it into the shop to work on it. We had a new engine installed, had all the dents removed and painted it with the current 1989 paint scheme. We had all the seats removed, and had new floor mats put in. An upholstery shop picked up all the seats and reupholstered them. Then they reinstalled them after the new mats were installed. The Chevrolet dealership did an extraordinary job. When they finished with it, it even smelled like a brand-new car. The Navajos that had been riding in it for several years did not recognize it. They asked me, "Is it a new car?"

My dad died on March 14, 1989. The funeral was on the 17th at Cielo Vista Baptist Church in El Paso, Texas. Harriett and I made two trips to El Paso to help settle my father's affairs. Mom moved in with my sister in Tornillo, Texas.

In early 1989, the Navajo Nation almost seemed like a third world country with a political and sometimes physical battle to see who would wind up in control. The Chairman of the Navajo Nation (the Chief) had been accused of graft and corruption by a Senate investigating committee. The Tribal Council voted him out of office but the fight continued. Tensions came to the boiling point on July 20th, and violence erupted in Window Rock. A mob, armed with clubs, incited by the former Chairman of the Navajo Tribe, attempted to reinstate him by force. In the confrontation with Tribal police, two men were killed and many injured. It was anarchy pure and simple. It almost came to the point where martial law was declared and federal marshals being called in to restore order. The Chairman was sentenced to prison where he remained until President Clinton pardoned him when he left office.

The first week of June, we held our annual Daily Vacation Bible School. The Chapter House provided summertime meals for kids each day at noon. We coordinated with them, had our Bible classes, then took the kids for their hot lunch, and then took them home. It was a win all the way around. The Chapter House had a larger attendance because they had someone bring the children for their meals and the children got fed a hot meal after going to the Bible school. That year we registered 78 children and 16 were saved.

My mother only lived for three months after my father's death. She was diagnosed with terminal cancer and only lived two weeks after she was diagnosed. They are buried side by side and are together again with the Lord. I just thank the Lord for the good parents I had, and the things they taught me as I was growing up. To them, their kids always came first. They were always there for me and always gave me unconditional love. They were able to visit us in the Philippines and then several times on the Navajo Indian Reservation.

The Suburban my dad had found for me in El Paso had also worn out. The roads were just hard on vehicles. The four-wheel drive was used almost every mile we drove. I had been going to government auctions trying to buy another Suburban but I was always about $1,000 short on what they sold for. Pastor Bill Woodward, Central Baptist Church, Black Creek, New York sent word that they would donate a 15-passenger maxi-van for us to use on the Reservation if we could come and get it. They warned us that it was not running and it was very rusty from being driven over roads that had been salted.

Our daughter Gloria, and her husband Lowell Haggerty had just finished helping with the church Fellowship Hall. The church in New York was about 200 miles past their church in Ohio. We decided to follow them back to Ohio in our car, and then go to New York and pick up the maxi-van. Lowell and I went from Ohio to pick up the van. Lowell, being an expert mechanic, had it running in no time, but all the lower paneling was rusted away. We drove it back to Lake Milton, Ohio and put it in the church's bus barn to work on it. Pastor Jim White, of a neighboring church provided new

111

lower siding and Lowell cut off the rusted siding and replaced it. A church in Cincinnati donated $1,000 to buy parts and the van was reconditioned and repainted. Harriett and I drove it and our car back to the Reservation and we put it to work hauling Navajos. It earned its keep over and over.

We left the Reservation on September 4th to go for the van, and as it had been almost five years since we started working with the Navajos, we decided to take several months to have a short furlough and report to churches. We planned on returning to pick up our mail once a month. We reported to churches in Ohio and Texas during that period of furlough. Brother Marvin Long, our Navajo preacher, took charge of the ministry while we were away.

## Chapter 12 – **Second Term on the Reservation**

We returned from our short furlough in December, 1989. We were blessed as the Navajos were now taking a much bigger role in the ministry reflecting their growth as Christians. The results for 1989 was 40 saved and two surrendered their lives. As the new year started, we continued for a while to report to churches and work at Crystal at the same time. During February, I reported to two churches and preached at Crystal two Sundays.

In the summer of 1990, Eastland Baptist Church made our cup to run over. The young people, under the youth director, Bill Fields, came and conducted a Daily Vacation Bible School. Brother David Hardy came at the same time, plus several other men who were carpenters and cement men. Brother Jim Ramsey and his wife, Linda, came to help with the music ministry. We set up the revival tent and used it plus the church to hold the DVBS. Then in the evenings, Brother Hardy preached a revival in the tent. The men who came did a lot of cement work, built an enclosed porch onto our mobile home, and painted the 50' office trailer. The BIA boarding school loaned us about 200 chairs and a portable platform to put in the revival tent. Brother Fields used Eastland's big bus to haul kids from the town of Navajo.

The young people who came to the DVBS in the morning wanted to come back at night, so Eastland's young people taught them both morning and in the evening. On one of the first days, I sat at the back of the auditorium and listened to Brother John Mardirosian, who was about 16 years of age, teach the older Navajo young people. When he gave the invitation, there were 10 saved. Wednesday evening the attendance reached 250. The combined results of the tent revival and the DVBS was 67 saved!! That was a week to remember.

Staying warm in the winter time was something we had to take seriously. July and August were months when we gathered wood to save on the cost of propane. Our home and the church had both propane furnaces and wood stoves. To use just propane would have been too expensive. In our home, we used wood during the hours we were awake. At night we would turn the thermostat down to 55 degrees and use lots of cover. The next morning one of us would get up and get the fire going in the wood stove, and turn up the thermostat for the central heat, to warm the place up. Even taking these precautions, we still used about 200 gallons of propane a month during the winter months. At the church, we kept the thermostat just high enough that the water pipes would not freeze, and we would also use 200 gallons of propane there also.

On a typical weekend, I would work most of Saturday using a snow blower trying to get the parking lot where it would be usable. Then, hopefully, the tribe would grade the road in front of the church. Extreme cold did not keep the Navajo people from coming to church. On December 23, 1990, the temperature was 30 degrees below zero, and the building was almost completely filled. It made me wonder, if we had a church of Anglos, how many would have been there. Navajos are tough.

In the summer of 1991, Bellmead Calvary Baptist Church's young people came to the Reservation and put on a DVBS. Their youth director had made them earn the right to come on the trip by memorizing verses and learning how to lead someone to the Lord. As a result, they had 26 Navajo young people saved. Pastor Adams later told me when his young people came home they were walking on air and several of them surrendered their lives to do the Lord's will. There is a big difference in reading the words, *"Lift up your eyes, and look on the fields; for they are white already to harvest,"* and being there and seeing them for yourself.

The next week after our DVBS, Harriett and I were missionary speakers at Park Hill Baptist Church's DVBS in Pueblo, Colorado. Both Harriett and I taught missionary stories during the Bible school, and I was asked to draw the net. The Lord blessed with 32 children saved there and several surrendering their lives. Then on Sunday, two more were saved. Park Hill had a contest, pitting the boys against the girls in who could bring the most pennies. There was a big balance scale to find who had brought the most. They converted the coin for check and gave us the $750 collected in pennies that week.

Raymond Mullahon was an alcoholic when I first met him. He and his wife, Lina, were members of the Mormon church. Lina had been raised in a Mormon family and, after their marriage, had been instrumental in getting Raymond into the Mormon church.

One day, as I was coming out of the Crystal Trading Post, I saw Raymond working on his Chevrolet automobile. I walked over and watched for a moment, and then asked Raymond what was wrong. He answered, "I think it is the fuel pump." I noticed that his Chevy had a 350 engine, and I remembered that I had a new fuel pump for a 350 engine in my storeroom. I had bought it for one of our Suburbans and then found out the problem was a hole in the gasoline line instead of the fuel pump. God touched my heart to give Raymond the fuel pump. I told Raymond, "If you find out it is really the fuel pump, I have one in my storeroom that I will give you." Then I left and went back home.

About an hour later, Raymond came to my house and said, "Mr. Carter, I know it's the fuel pump because gasoline is running out of it." So, I went to the storeroom and got the fuel pump for him. It was a new fuel pump and still in the original box with the price I had paid marked on the box.

When I handed it to him, he asked, "How much money do I owe you?" I answered, "You don't owe me anything. I told you I would give it to you if it will fit your car. The only thing I ask is that if it will not work, bring it back so I can give it to someone else." Raymond thanked me for the fuel pump and then left to install it on his car. Afterward, I saw him driving his car around Crystal, so I knew it worked.

Raymond had been to our church a couple of times, because he had a sister and two brothers who were members, but his wife, Lina, had never come. The next Sunday after giving Raymond the fuel pump, Raymond, Lina, and the children showed up for church. I was really surprised to see Lina come to the Baptist church.

They came regularly for several weeks, and then one Sunday evening after the services, everyone else left but the Mullahons. My wife, Harriett, and I were sitting on the back pew in the church visiting with them. The talk got to spiritual things and then I asked Lina, "Lina, would you like to be saved?" She said, "I sure would."

Then we knelt down there by the back pew, and I showed her in the Bible how to be saved, and she accepted Christ as her own personal Savior. When we were finished, I looked at Raymond and big tears were running down his cheeks. He said, "What about me, Pastor Carter?" I told him, "You're next, Raymond." The two of us went to the altar and in a short while he was receiving Jesus into his heart.

The Mullahons became faithful members of Baptist Bible Navajo Church. Raymond never took another drink and soon Lina was one of our Sunday School teachers. Also, it wasn't long until Lina had won almost all of her Mormon family to the Lord. Then God touched Raymond's heart with the call to preach. It came at a good time as Marvin Long had resigned as associate pastor.

116

There followed several years of training for Raymond on site at the church. I would make him a copy of the message I was preaching so he could see how I developed the sermons. Gradually, he was asked to preach more and more. I was always blessed with his messages. They were not rehashes of my old sermons, but he was getting his messages the same place I was getting them, straight from the Lord.

In 1994, the church voted for Raymond to be their pastor with a 100% vote. Not even one no vote. Raymond testified later that he thought that after he was saved, all he would be doing is going to church and listening to the preaching and teaching. He had no idea that God was going to use him to be a preacher to his own Navajo people.

Now, when I think back, I praise the Lord for the return on the investment of a fuel pump for an old Chevy car. God touched my heart to give a Mormon a fuel pump bought with Baptist money. God touched Raymond's heart that an Anglo missionary loved him because he gave him the fuel pump with no strings attached. When we follow God's leading, we can never go wrong.

God tested Raymond's faith in the fall of 1991. While both Raymond and Lina were working and their children were at school, their house burned to the ground. They lost all their household belongings, all their clothes with the exception of what they were wearing, and all the books I was using to train him for the ministry. He passed the test with flying colors, and God blessed him. As a Navajo veteran, he was given all the material to build a nice house. He just had to build it himself.

God also blessed Harriett and I. It had been 25 years since God called us to be His missionaries. We counted 60 saved on the

Reservation in 1991, and Raymond had really developed as a preacher. It blessed my heart to hear him preach.

In the Philippines, due to the tropical heat, it was imperative that we took a vacation every year. We did not continue that while on the Navajo Indian Reservation. After seven years on the Reservation, we took our first vacation in May, 1992. We went to a family reunion, and visited all our children, and went to Mineral Wells, Texas to see our granddaughter, Michelle Bice, graduate from High School. Michelle was born while we were working in the Philippine Islands. We drove a lot of miles, but getting to visit all our family made it worth it.

The church also had a great summer with a good DVBS and a good spirit in the church. There were 40 saved, several baptized, and two grandkids, Jacob Carter and Melanie Bice, came and stayed almost a month. They were both 15 years of age. I used the dirt roads around our church to teach them to drive my Suburban, and also taught them the basics of how to fly an airplane. I could not let them solo as they lacked one year being old enough for a student pilot license. I had them to the point where I would have soloed them if they had been old enough.

When it was time for them to go home, we used the airplane and I let them fly left seat. Jacob flew from Window Rock, Arizona to Tucumcari, New Mexico where we refueled. Then Melanie flew to Mineral Wells, Texas, because she wanted her parents to see her land the airplane. Jacob then flew to Tulsa, Oklahoma because his dad, Mike, was living in Sapulpa.

When we had DVBS, on the last day, we invited the parents to come to an evening service where we gave the children their awards. One parent came and heard about salvation. A few days later, I was driving toward our church from visitation and I saw the parent by the side of the road waving for me to stop. When I stopped, he said, "Pastor Carter, I want you to save me." I answered, "I cannot save you." He looked confused. I said, "I cannot save you, but I can introduce you to Jesus, the One who can save you." He got in the vehicle with me, we went to the church and knelt down at the altar, and the parent got saved. I wanted him to know for certain it wasn't the missionary, it was the missionary's God who was in the saving business.

By December, 1992, there was already about two feet of snow on the ground. I had to shovel out paths to the office, from the cars to the house, and to the church. Also, at the Boarding School next door, we taught a religion class and had eight Navajo students accept Christ as their Savior.

January,1993, started with a bang, or maybe I should say back to back snow storms. At Crystal, it snowed eleven straight days. Our area was declared a disaster area and the National Guard was called in to deliver food for people and hay for animals. They used helicopters to deliver it. On my birthday, January 17, it was impossible to have services because the roads were impassable. There were five-foot drifts across the road on both sides of our home. This was one of the few times that we had to cancel church.

On Wednesday the 20th, as Harriett and I were picking up people in the Suburban we slid into a deep ditch and became stranded. The road grader had graded the road and his blade had strayed from the road until the right side of the plowed part was over the ditch. I got too close and down in the ditch we went. The snow on the right side of the Suburban came all the way up to the middle of the right passenger window. That is about five feet deep. We were stuck there until it was too late to have church. Finally, a Navajo lady came by in a big pickup truck. She had a heavy-duty nylon tow rope. I dug down and attached it to a hook under my front bumper. When she started to pull, the nylon tow rope stretched for a while and then when the Suburban started to move it began to retract and shot us right out of that ditch. Then on Sunday, the church was packed. I preached a sermon, "What to do When the Devil Knocks You Down" and the altars were filled. You just have to get up one more time than you are knocked down. The mud and snow were just obstacles that had to be overcome in order to have victory.

In February, the temperature rose above freezing during the daylight hours. Melting snow along with rain made the roads impassable without four-wheel drive. I used our Suburban to pull vehicles out of the mud, and also to transport some of the people of our community in emergencies. A few times they would park their vehicles at the Trading Post and I would take them on home.

We did not have a good year health wise. Harriett's annual mammogram came up positive and she had a biopsy to remove the lump. Two days after the surgery, I took some kind of virus and two days later I collapsed at home. Harriett had to get out of her sick bed to drive me to the doctor. We were sitting in the exam room when I began to feel faint. I told the doctor, "I am about to leave you now." He said, "You can't faint sitting up." But I did. Next thing I remember, I was on the examining table with the doctor working on me. He put me in the hospital. He said, "I am tired of you scaring Harriett." I was in the hospital only two days, but it took both of us a good while to recover.

In the Spring of 1993, there was an outbreak of some mysterious flu-like disease that was killing young, healthy adults. The victims of this disease had mostly all been from on or immediately around the Navajo Reservation. Crystal, where we lived, was in the middle of the area where the disease had struck, but none of our members were affected.

The tent revival, the one where we had the Navajo Code Talker, was held on June 7$^{th}$ to the 13$^{th}$. The weather did not cooperate. The first day of the revival there was ice on the tent where it had frozen the night before. (And this was in June.) We put all the sides down on the tent and then used kerosene heaters inside the tent. The Navajos wore several layers of clothing and then brought blankets to wrap up in. It reminded me of old time pictures I had seen of Indians wrapped in blankets. The blankets kept them warm in old times and they still kept them warm. The weather was cold, but Brother Roy Hawthorne's preaching was hot and as a result six were saved.

Sickness plagued us that fall. Harriett fell and broke her shoulder. Then she had the flu, which wound up being double pneumonia. Just as she got back on her feet, I got sick and was in bed for a week.

Christmas day came and the Carters were home alone. None of our family could come to the Reservation, and we were not able to go to any of our kin folks. About 10am, Raymond Mullahon dropped by to visit for a little while. As he left he said, "Brother Carter, could you and Mrs. Carter come to my house in an hour or two?" After he left, I told Harriett, "I think we've just been invited to Christmas dinner." We pulled some ice cream out of the freezer to have something to contribute, and went to Raymond's house. There was a total of 26 of us there, and Lina had cooked a turkey, a ham, and all the other things that make up a good dinner. We thoroughly enjoyed the meal and the company. Harriett told me on the way home, "I feel like I just had Christmas dinner with family." She was right, they really were our family.

The disease that struck last year and killed many Navajos had caused some of the churches that normally send young people to the Reservation to hold DVBS classes to have second thoughts. No one should willingly send their young people into a danger zone. We were going to do our DVBS with just our Navajo people, but I got a call from a MK (missionary kid) from the Philippines. The call was from Dawn Waters, daughter of Larry and Mary Waters, our dear friends from the Philippines. She had graduated from High School and was now Stateside and wanted to come visit. Her visit would coincide with the DVBS and she wanted to teach one of the classes. She was visiting her uncle who was a scientist at Los Alamos, New Mexico. I planned to pick her up with the airplane.

As the airport at Los Alamos is a Department of Defense airport, I asked her uncle if I would need a special permit to land there, and was told that I would not. When I arrived to pick her up and called the airport, I found that I did need a special permit. When I was refused permission to land, I asked if they would inform the one I was to pick up to go to Santa Fe, New Mexico and I would pick her up there. I suppose the uncle pulled some rank, because they called me back and gave me a special permit number, and I was able to land and meet Dawn's uncle and grandmother. I then loaded Dawn aboard the airplane and flew her to the Navajo Reservation.

God blessed her teaching at the DVBS and she wound up the week with 10 saved in her class. The Navajo elders were impressed that she would come during a time when so many were afraid to come. Brother Raymond Mullahon led the church to buy her a Navajo handmade bracelet with ten turquoise stones to represent the ten souls that were saved through her teaching.

The last day of the DVBS, I was going to preach a final message to the children and draw the net for salvation. Before this, as I was waiting, my dog at my house across the street was barking at me over at the church. When I would look at him, he would look back over his shoulder as if to tell me, there is something over here you need to take care of. I wondered if someone had gotten into my shop and I went to check. What had happened was that a hummingbird had flown into my enclosed porch and could not find his way back out. The bird was flying into the window trying to escape and was worn completely out. I caught the hummingbird and put my finger under its little feet. Then I carried him out from under the porch. I then opened my hand so he could be free. He began to fly away and got higher and higher as he flew to a tree about 50 yards away. God had given me an illustration of salvation for my message. Just like the hummingbird, man is trapped by sin. He can't help himself. He cannot escape. But Jesus comes in. He rescues us from the slave market of sin and sets us free. Then we can climb higher and higher just like the little hummingbird. I related this story in my message and several were saved.

When you take the offensive against Satan, you can expect him to fight back. Within a week of the close of our DVBS, I received a death threat from a man who said he was a servant of Satan. It bothered me for an hour or two, but it just reminded me to put on the whole armor of God. The Bible promises that if I have it on I can stand.

Thanksgiving Day is a time of remembrance. We started a tradition for several of the missionary families to get together for Thanksgiving each year. For several years we had all met at the home of Missionary Scott Merritt. Once we had all sat down at the table loaded down with goodies, Mrs. Carrie Merritt had each one seated around the table to share with the rest some of the things we were thankful for that had happened during the past year. Needless to say, we all rejoiced together.

As 1994 came to a close, we estimated 50 souls saved for the year. We were also becoming concerned because of our age, now 66, and with great-grandchildren, and the danger of the severe conditions we lived under most of the year. We never left the house in our vehicle without a survival kit inside. I had a fear that if one of us fell and broke a leg, the other could not get them up and to safety. Baptist Bible Navajo Church now had its own pastor. If we started another church, it would take 10 years to have it where we could turn it over to its own pastor. By that time, we would be over 75 years of age. Brother David Hardy, our sending pastor, had been advising retirement, but I wanted the Lord to tell me what to do.

The Lord spoke to my heart and we decided to retire in August, 1995. I would not retire from preaching, just from being a missionary. I bought a home in Oologah, Oklahoma, not too far from Tulsa. Until I retired my granddaughter, Donna Edwards, lived in it. The Mission Office informed us that we could continue our medical insurance as long as we raised enough money to make the payments. We had signed up for social security and Medicare when we reached 65 years of age.

Temple Baptist Church of Odessa, Texas sent its young people to conduct our DVBS in 1995. They did a great job and 52 Navajo young people made a profession of faith. DVBS over the years was a time of reaping on the Reservation.

On Friday, July 7th, I taught finances at the church of Missionary Scott Merritt. I was very sick when I left there to go home. After getting home I kept getting worse. Finally, Harriett called an ambulance to take me to the hospital. I was so out of it that young people from our church who were emergency workers helped me out of bed and into the ambulance and I did not know it. I was brought to the Indian Hospital in Window Rock where they found that I had E. coli in my bloodstream. I remained in the ER in the Indian hospital until I could be cleared to be sent to Gallup. I was hospitalized for one week.

The first of August, I sold my Cherokee 180 airplane and turned it over to its new owner. Back a couple of years before God called me to be a missionary, He had told me to sell the airplane I then owned and buy church bonds. I explained earlier how He allowed me to use that money over and over again. Later, he allowed me to fly again with the airplanes of Fellowship Aviation Supply and Training, and then my son-in-law's airplane. I used the Maule on the Reservation until I was able to buy the Cherokee 180. The Cherokee paid its own way through the flight training it did, and when I sold it, I made a profit of $14,000. God is so good. He allowed me to enjoy my love of flying at little or no cost.

At the beginning of August my daughter, Sandra, and her husband, R. L. Brown came to the Reservation to help us pack and move. We rented a large U-Haul truck and packed it full. It was so hard to say "Goodbye" to all our dear Navajo friends. Our last Sunday at church, they gave us a surprise meal with all our favorite Navajo foods. Then the night before we left, the folks at the Chapter House (the local seat of government on the Reservation) gave a party in our honor. The ladies of the community had even quilted a hand sewn quilt for Harriett and me, which they presented at the party. It surprised me when different ones made speeches about what our coming to the Reservation had meant to them. Many of the people there were not members of our church, but many were. One young man told how he became a Christian. I had come by his house and invited him to our DVBS. He said he attended and got saved. Another lady, who was not a member said, "We can see God's love through Pastor Carter." I was humbled.

The Navajo Indian Reservation was the safest place I have ever lived, in terms of violence. More than ten years and nothing at all was ever stolen. In the latter years, Navajo men would drive the Suburban and maxi-van to pick up people for church. We just left the keys in the ash trays. Try that anywhere else and your vehicle would be long gone.

Before daylight the next day, we left for Oklahoma. It did not start out well. Before we got to Gallup, the muffler fell off the diesel U-Haul truck we had rented. Talk about something making a lot of noise, a diesel engine without a muffler will curdle bird's eggs in their nests for a half a mile. We stopped in Albuquerque to have it repaired and had to spend the night.

## Chapter 13 – **After the Mission Field**

We had lived for more than ten years at almost 8,000 feet in altitude. Thin air, cool nights, and balmy days was what we had become acclimatized to. We moved to Oklahoma in August, in the middle of the hottest season of the year. Sweat poured from me in buckets as I worked unloading the truck. I found out what headbands are for. I could take one off and wring the sweat out of it. When I came to Oklahoma from the Philippines, I thought it was a cold place, and when I came to Oklahoma from the Reservation I thought it was a hot place. You become acclimatized to where you have been living.

Two weeks after moving to Oklahoma, Pastor Harlan Chute had me preach as veteran missionary at his mission conference in Sperry, Oklahoma. It felt good to further the cause for missions.

In the next three months, we were in six mission conferences and had seen God's people promise $400,000 in faith promise mission giving, plus several who had surrendered their lives. One of our mission conferences was back on the Navajo Reservation at Mentmore with Missionary Ted Farris. We got to see many of our old church members, as they drove 50 miles, one way, to come to the conference.

Back home in Oklahoma, one evening in April, I woke up with chills and fever. I went to the doctor the next day, and found that I had another case of E. coli in my blood, just as I had the year before on the Reservation. I was in Intensive Care for two days.

In May, Harriett and I celebrated our 50th wedding anniversary. Our children made it a special time and gave a reception at the Eastland Baptist Church Family Center. Several hundred people came from at least six states. There were missionaries, pastors, friends and families there. There were even three of our four great-grandchildren there. We were so honored.

After the reception, we took a travel trailer, our oldest daughter, Gloria, and her husband, Pastor Lowell Haggerty, and a couple from their church in Ohio, Dale and Betty Lou Williams, and spent about six days in Yellowstone National Park. It was a fun time. It was too early in the season for there to be the huge crowds yet. We saw lots of wildlife and lots of snow. After visiting Yellowstone National Park, we went to the Grand Teton National Park. In the Grand Teton Park there is a chapel that has the back wall made of glass. It is a popular place to have weddings as the beautiful Teton Mountains are visible through the glass wall. As it was Sunday morning, we decided to have church. We voted for Pastor Haggerty to preach and we sat down for our worship service. Other visitors to the Park would come in, see the services going on, and have a seat. We not only had an opportunity to worship, we had an opportunity to witness to others.

In July, I got a call from Raymond Mullahon, the pastor of Baptist Bible Navajo Church, informing me of the death of his brother, and asking me to come back to the Reservation to preach the funeral. Their Mission Conference started right after the funeral so we stayed for that. There were two Navajo ladies saved during the conference. Then Mrs. Mary Yazzie, one of the dear old ladies of the church died, and her daughter asked me to conduct the funeral. We were also doing hospital visitation. I told Harriett it was just like coming off a furlough instead of just being there on a visit.

When we first left the mission field, we moved to Oologah, Oklahoma. It just did not work out living there. It was a long drive to go to Eastland Baptist Church, which I made almost daily doing different jobs around the church. For a short time, I was voted president of the Fellowship Aviation Supply and Training, and I, along with other volunteers, did construction work making an office and a place to work on airplanes. I just did not fit in at that leadership position. I was not the man for the job. It just wasn't my calling. I resigned that position after about six months, although I kept flying, mostly as an instructor. I gave the pilots their required bi-annual flight reviews and their instrument currency checks.

One day I received a call from my daughter, Sandra Brown, telling me that the house directly behind them in Owasso, Oklahoma, was going to be sold at a sheriff's sale at the courthouse. There were lots of pluses. It was next door to family and we could look out for one another. It was a lot closer to our church, Eastland Baptist. I enlisted the help of Mrs. Grace Hardy, who worked in real estate, and bought the house at auction. Then came the cleanup. The house had not been lived in for a year, the back yard was waist high in weeds, and it was badly in need of repairs and a paint job.

Brother Eddie Gerodias and his wife Inday, had been flown to the States by a church in Louisiana to preach an evangelistic meeting. Brother Eddie had agreed to come with the provision that he would be able to come visit his missionaries, the Carters. Eddie and Inday spent a couple of weeks with us. When they found out we had the house in Owasso that needed painting, they volunteered to help us paint the house. Their help was invaluable, and we got in a lot of visiting while we worked. In September, 1996, we moved into our home in Owasso.

Our next project was to build a building in the back yard for a wood workshop. After building on churches for years, wood-working had become my hobby. I needed a place to install all the wood tools I had acquired over the years since returning from the Philippines. We first dug the foundation for a 24' X 24' building

129

and then men from Eastland Baptist came out and did all the cement work. I ordered roof trusses already made, Harriett and I made the walls, and then the Eastland men came back out and set them all up. We had metal siding and roof installed and insulated it so it could be heated and cooled and used winter and summer. Job done.

I was unhappy about one thing in our house in Owasso. It had a fireplace. I was fed up with cutting wood and feeding a fire from all the years in Crystal where it was an absolute necessity. It was cold all around the fireplace, and I called it a pneumonia hole. R. L. Brown, my son-in-law, told me that we could remove the fireplace so that became our next project. After taking out the fireplace, we rebuilt the entire wall including putting in a lot of insulation. We put in drywall and textured it and painted it. Now we had a warm living room with a lot of extra space. R. L. is a master carpenter.

In April, 1997, Brother David Hardy flew the FAST Cessna 205 to a Fellowship Meeting in Amarillo, Texas. The weather deteriorated until he had to leave the airplane and borrow a van to come home in. He asked me to return the van and pick up the airplane when the weather got better. The church needed their van back, so sooner was better than later. I asked Brother Don Stroud to make the trip with me to help with the driving and flying. He in turn asked Peter Davidson, an eleven-year-old boy in our church that Brother Stroud knew was interested in flying, to go with us. The airplane was at the Downtown Airpark in Amarillo.

Everything went well returning the van until we were about 30 miles from Amarillo, where we ran into rain. The church that owned the van told us to take it to the airport and when we left just lock the keys inside as they had another set of keys. The weather continued to deteriorate and the wind got stronger. Brother Stroud handled the call for weather and the filing of the IFR flight plan. He was told we would run out of the clouds after about 30 or 40 miles. I was to fly the airplane and Brother Stroud was to navigate and do the radio work.

By the time we had the airplane running, the ceiling was 100 feet and the wind was blowing right down the runway at 37 knots. I taxied to the end of the runway and when clear for takeoff taxied onto the runway. I advanced the throttle, released the brakes and we started rolling. Almost immediately with the high headwind we were at flying speed. When I pulled back on the wheel, we were instantly in the clouds and I started climbing for altitude. When Brother Stroud called the air controllers and reported our take-off time, conditions had changed. There were tornados along our intended flight path. It was decided that we would fly north out of Amarillo into Kansas and then go east and then down to Tulsa. That was one flight that I was happy to have two pilots in the cockpit.

During 1997, I had been preaching every chance I got filling pulpits and preaching mission conferences. About the first of September, I was asked to fill in at Claremore Baptist Temple on a Wednesday evening. After the service, the men asked me for advice on how to call a pastor. There were only about 10 folks present at the Wednesday service. I asked them how many they had on Sundays. They told me the same ten that were there would be all they had coming. I did not see how they could afford to call a pastor with just three or four families. God touched my heart. And I offered to be their interim pastor, without pay, until we could get the church built up enough to call a full-time pastor. The next Wednesday, they had a business meeting and called me to be their interim pastor. The 21st of September was my first Sunday to preach as their pastor.

I started out just like I did on the mission field, by preaching doctrinal sermons to be sure everyone was solidly grounded. The church was supporting 17 or 18 missionaries at $50 per month, so tithing and mission giving was emphasized. I was interim pastor for nine months and the church kept up their missionary commitment every month.

I very much enjoyed pastoring Claremore Baptist Temple as I had felt lost not preaching on a constant basis, but they needed someone younger with more energy than me. By the following April, the attendance was running around 50. All bills and all missionaries were paid and we had a surplus of $12,000 in the bank. The church called a permanent pastor, Steve Marcaurelle, who would take over his duties at the end of May.

With my work at Claremore Baptist Temple finished, I was clear to accept a challenge from Missionary Ted Farris on the Navajo Indian Reservation. He asked me to take over his work while he took a short furlough to report to his churches. This would be a chance to be used of the Lord, and to again minister to the Navajo people that we loved so dearly.

In July, we left for the Reservation with "walking pneumonia" and we felt terrible. Mentmore, where Brother Farris has his church is near Gallup. One of the Gallup doctors, Dr. James Whitfield, was a close friend and on his way to his office in the morning he would come by our house and check on Harriett and me. It took several weeks for us to feel normal again but we recovered. Brother Farris' wife, Toni, was the pianist, and no one else could play the piano. I went to a pawn shop and bought a guitar which I played while I led the singing.

Being back on the mission field felt like we had come home. We fell right back into the groove of missionary work just as if we had never left. The attendance was good and the offerings were great. Pastor Farris had these folks well grounded. Two adult Navajos accepted Christ as their Savior. I was able to win one man to the Lord in the surgery waiting room while his wife was undergoing surgery. His wife and son came to the Mentmore church, and his son had been praying for his father to be saved ever since I had been there. Praise the Lord, his prayers were answered.

One Sunday evening we had a special treat. Pastor Mullahon brought the entire Baptist Bible Navajo Church of Crystal to the Grace Navajo Baptist Church of Mentmore for combined evening services. It was so good to see all our old members again. After the service, we all went to a Chinese buffet in Gallup and had dinner together. Then in the parking lot when we parted, it must have been a shock to people who saw us. They were probably wondering why all those Navajos were hugging two old white people.

On October 21$^{st}$ until the 25$^{th}$, the annual mission conference was held. The year before the Mentmore church had promised $12, 900 for missions and actually gave $13,262.29. This time the promise was $14,025.60. Their faith had increased. Also, there was one saved during the mission conference.

One day, someone knocked on the door. I opened to find some ladies there that had once attended Grace Navajo Baptist Church. The father of the family was a Peyote priest who had stopped his family from coming to the church. Some of the children had been saved and baptized, but the mother had never made a public profession. They told me their mother had died. These were the ones who had been saved, and they asked me to conduct the funeral. It was an opportunity to preach to a lot of lost people at the same time, even though some would be hostile. I agreed to conduct the services. There were about 300 people at the funeral services. The funeral home auditorium was overflowing and people were standing at the sides and in the halls. I preached a gospel message and gave an invitation. I told them I was going to pray a "sinner's prayer" and if they wanted to be saved to silently pray the same prayer along with me. Then I asked for a show of hands of those who had prayed with me. There were 14 people saved!! As I stood at the head of the casket as people filed by, I could tell who had enjoyed the message and who had hated it. Some would shake my hand and thank me for the message while others stalked by with their hands clasped behind their backs. The Bible tells us to be instant, in season, out of season.

Toward the end of 1998, Brother and Sister Farris returned from their furlough to their mission field. We had a special "Welcome Home Missionary" day in honor of their return. It was a stormy day with snow in the air and snow on the ground. In the morning service, the attendance was 111, and in the evening service, an attendance of 90! During our time there, 18 Navajos had made their way to the altar to ask the Lord to save their souls. We returned to Tulsa just before Christmas.

In 1999, I was in a quandary, wondering whether to teach a regular Sunday School class, or to keep Sundays open to fill pulpits or preach mission conferences. I had cataract surgery that did not go well. I began to have double vision, with Harriett having to do the driving. Pastor Hardy had asked me to teach doctrine to the Senior Citizens class, that at that time was called the "Pioneers." I had resigned myself to the double vision but Loran Winfield, one of the members of the class told me about a doctor in Midwest City he thought could help me. Loran and Doris even drove us down for the appointment. Their doctor sent me to a neuro-ophthalmologist, a Dr. Farris. He won my heart immediately, when he began by saying he liked to pray for his patients before examining them.

After one of the most thorough eye exams I had ever had, Dr. Farris prescribed some glasses that cured my double vision. He also brought back a lot of the sight in the eye that had been damaged by the cataract surgery. I could now see 20/20 and Harriett was proud she did not have to do all the driving. Also, I could fly again. Brother Don Stroud brought me back up to date with flight training until I was proficient again.

I was still preaching at every available opportunity. I also was preaching in a nursing home in Tulsa on a regular basis. In the year 1999, I preached in several mission conferences where over $300,000 was promised for missions.

In the fall of 2000, I became a volunteer professor at Heartland Baptist Bible College in Oklahoma City. Because of the 250-mile round-trip distance to the college, all my classes were on one day of the week. That way I only had to make the trip once a week unless there was something special going on.

I had anticipated they would want me to teach missions, but that was already covered. I was asked to teach Bible. Over different years, I taught 1st and 2nd Corinthians, James, Galatians, and Revelation. Plus, I taught a 4th year theology class called Dispensationalism.

Teaching students was not new to me as I had taught at the Bible college in Cebu, and had founded and taught in the Bacolod Bible Baptist Seminary. But there is a great responsibility in teaching tomorrows pastors and missionaries. I felt the need for more teaching myself, and I enrolled in a correspondence course in the Louisiana Baptist University. Brother Roy Wallace was my mentor. The very same Roy Wallace who preached at our church in Calatrava, Philippines, where the people stood out in the rain to hear him preach. In the Spring of 2005, I earned my PHD. My senior

135

thesis was entitled, "Unveiling the Book of Revelation." I then had the thesis published, and it became the textbook for my class on Revelation at Heartland. The things I learned, I was able to pass along through my classes at Heartland.

I taught at Heartland for a total of seven years before I could no longer make the trip down each week. Hopefully, I passed on my vision of soulwinning and building churches to a lot of my students who are now out in the real world doing business for God. I still meet former students who are now missionaries and pastors who thank me for teaching them.

In June, 2001, some of the workers at Eastland were going to Crystal to conduct their DVBS. I decided I would fly out and get things ready for them to come. Don Stroud loaned me his Cherokee PA-28-160 for the trip. Peter Davidson, who was now taking a private pilot course with Brother Stroud, went along to get some cross-country time and to help when we got there. He was also going to join the youth group that was coming by bus and help with the DVBS. I would fly back solo before the DVBS was over.

We flew out of Harvey Young airport and landed in Amarillo. When we got out of the plane we could hear birds, but we could see no birds. It sounded as if the birds were inside the airplane. Then we discovered there was a bird nest in the fuselage of our airplane. We had to rescue the birds before we could continue our trip. Our next stop was Grants, New Mexico because we needed fuel. Leaving Grants, Peter learned about high density altitude. After he took off, he tried to use the same angle of climb that he did in Tulsa. I told him to watch his airspeed and reduce his angle of attack. When that was corrected the airplane climbed, but at a lot slower rate than if we had been at low altitude. The density altitude must have been about 10,000 feet. Peter said he learned a valuable lesson.

We parked the airplane in Gallup, and Missionary Ted Farris picked us up and let us stay in his mission apartment overnight. Then he loaned us a vehicle and I borrowed a mower to use at Crystal. When we got to Crystal, we mowed the church yard and got things ready for the DVBS. After the workers from Eastland arrived, Peter rejoined them and I returned Brother Stroud's airplane to Tulsa.

For the next several years, in my spare time, I was Peter Davidson's flight instructor as he worked to get his Instrument license, then his Commercial license, and then his Certified Flight Instructors license. I am very proud of the pilot he has become.

In 1998, Brother Troy Dorrell was added to the staff of Eastland Baptist Church. In 2003, Brother Hardy had pastored Eastland for 30 years. God led him to resign to let someone younger and with more energy take the lead. The church called Troy Dorrell as their new pastor. He has served the last 15 years. He is God's man for the job as the church has grown significantly under his leadership.

The real test for a missionary's work is will it continue after the missionary is gone. We started the church in San Carlos City in January 1973. The area became a flood zone because of indiscriminate building and bad city planning. The church had also outgrown the building. Pastor Eddie Gerodias had relocated and built a beautiful new church building. Its grand opening was January 26, 2003. Brother Eddie sent me the report for the day; 560 adults in attendance, 66 professions of faith, and 15 baptized. In addition, they raised 9,000 pesos for foreign missions on that special day.

I am so proud of the Philippine churches for the way they have propagated the gospel. They responded to my goal of 100 churches on the Island of Negros and exceeded that goal around 2008. I estimate approximately 120 churches there now. Their combined Sunday morning attendance on Negros is about 10,000, if they average near 80 each in attendance. Now they have extended their goals to foreign mission fields. The Filipinos that are going as missionaries and supported by Philippine churches now number in the hundreds.

In 2011, we were going to celebrate our 65$^{th}$ wedding anniversary, and I wanted to do something special. In our travels on deputation and furlough, we had traveled to all of the 50 states with the exception of Alaska. We decided to visit Alaska. Instead of taking a cruise to Alaska, we decided to fly to Fairbanks, get a hotel room, rent a car, and take some of the inland tours. We took one tour that took us by bus to the arctic circle. Along the way, the tour director took us to a place where they had dug a hole about a foot deep. We could reach down in the hole and feel the tundra, or permafrost where the subsoil is permanently frozen. To me, it felt like I was feeling a block of ice. We ate a picnic lunch right beside the Yukon River.

We drove our rental car from Fairbanks to the Denali National Park where we rode the tour bus deep into the park. We were able to see a lot of the wildlife, which included grizzly bears, moose, and caribou. We wanted to see Mt. McKinley, the tallest mountain on this continent, but the top remained hidden in the clouds.

We met some of the native Indians there in Alaska and found them to be almost like the Navajo people we had lived with. They are of the same language group, the Athabaskan, or as recently called, the Dene. They looked the same and their language was similar. It is thought the Navajo and Apache tribes migrated down from the Alaskan area and were relatively new comers to the southwest with their arrival in what is now Arizona and New Mexico about 1400 AD.

The time of the year we went to Alaska was in the summertime and it was daylight almost all the time. The sun would go down but it never got past twilight. I could take pictures at midnight with no flash. Our hotel room had heavy drapes so that people could sleep at night. Our first time to see night time was on the airliner flying back to the lower 48.

The Alaskan trip is now almost seven years ago and our 72$^{nd}$ wedding anniversary is coming up on May 16, 2018. God has been so good to us through all the years. The privilege of being called as a missionary exceeds anything I could have ever imagined.

At this point in my life, I now see God's plan for my life is as an encourager. Of course, I still try to encourage lost people to be saved, but now I feel my main job is to try to encourage God's people and encourage God's preachers and missionaries to be the best they can possibly be. Just as a football team is encouraged by the roar of the crowd, God's servants are encouraged when they hear the words, "Well done."

# Appendix

The Beechcraft Bonanza that God had me sell. The money was used over and over again in our training and ministry.

Mike operating the A.B. Dick Printing press in the Philippines.

The storefront church in San Carlos with pedicabs running past the church.

Our bus ministry was a motorcab ministry. The folks were brought in from the barrios.

All these standing by the motorcab rode in on the motorcab.

Children in front of the storefront church.

First baptism at San Carlos City. Nineteen new Babes in Christ.

Taping my radio program from the office in Cebu City.

Bible Baptist Church of San Carlos. Completed in 1974.

Bible Baptist Church of Calatrava. Our second church on the island of Negros.

Pastor & Mrs. Ugdiman. Persecuted for coming to church, he became a pastor.

Christmas tree made from a weed for Missionary Larry Water's children.

All these were riding in the one pickup plus the driver.

Inside Bible Baptist Church of Bacolod City.

Front of Bible Baptist Church of Bacolod City.

Boyd and Donna Lyons helping us in Bacolod.

Harriett rides a pedicab in San Carlos City.

Brother Hardy baptizing Filipinos in the Pacific Ocean.

Dave Hardy preaching to Bible Baptist Church at San Carlos.

College building at Bacolod City.

Choir at Bacolod church.

Crystal mission site lease from the air.

The Carters at Church at Crystal.

Maule airplane supplied by FAST Ministries to use on the Reservation.

DVBS held under the revival tent.

Revival meeting under the revival tent.

Jim Ramsey leading the singing at revival meeting.

Forty below zero at the Mission site at Crystal.

Barton Carter sitting in a Navajo hogan.

Marvin Long and Navajo children in church auditorium.

Building Fellowship Hall and SS rooms.

Fellowship Hall almost completed.

Inside Fellowship Hall with Harriett at the door.

Pastor and Lina Mullahon being baptized after receiving Christ.

Pastor Mullahon in full preacher mode.

Suburban after being rebuilt.

Made in the USA
Columbia, SC
02 March 2018